Beside the Still Waters is a seri
from book one of the Psalm
James Version). The psalms selected are the ones that the author believed the Lord wanted him to include.

These meditations were received through 'journalling'. That is, the author asked the Lord to talk to him about the psalms and then wrote down the thoughts that came into his mind as answers from Jesus and the Father. It should be remembered that we prophesy in part and that all prophecy should be judged. 1 Cor 13:9, 14:29.

By the same author

Come Away with Me – A prophetic meditation on the Song of Solomon

Beside the Still Waters

Prophetic meditations from book one of the Psalms

JONATHAN HINDSLEY

NATHANAEL BOOKS
Burnley

First published 2005

Published by Nathanael Books
c/o 27 Mosedale Drive, Burnley
Lancashire BB12 8UJ

ISBN 0 9545286 1 1

Book design and production for the publisher by
Bookprint Creative Services, P.O. Box 827,
BN21 3YJ, England.
Printed in Great Britain.

To the Holy Spirit – Who glorifies Jesus
for he takes of what is His and declares it to us.
Jn 16:14

Contents

Author's Note

In May 2000 I attended a conference at Revival Fires, Dudley, England when I heard Mark Virkler teach on 'Communion With God'. He introduced me to the idea that it was possible to tune to the flow of the Holy Spirit and write down what God was saying. As a 'left-brainer' I thought at first that this was not for me, but I decided to have a go anyway. To begin with I struggled a bit but then found to my surprise, that I did start hearing from the Lord. After the weekend I continued to experiment with 'journalling' and one day opened my Bible at the Song of Solomon. I decided to ask the Lord the question, 'Can You explain what it means for You to kiss me with the kisses of Your mouth?' The answer was the beginning of my book *Come Away With Me*. I decided to continue journalling in psalms and selected from book one, the ones that I felt that the Lord wished to speak about. The result is this book, and I hope that you are blessed, as I have been, as I share with you what I believe the Lord has said to me.

I would like to extend my thanks to Mark Virkler of Communion With God Ministries for teaching me how to 'tune to flow' and hear from God. Without his teaching this book would not have happened. I would also like to thank Sharon and Trevor Baker from Revival Fires for providing a well of refreshing at the Grace Centre, Dudley.

Mark Virkler can be contacted via www.cwgministries.org and Revival Fires via www.revivalfires.org.uk

Psalm One

Psalm 1:1

AUTHOR *Lord, what does it mean to be blessed?*

JESUS To be blessed is to have shalom – that is, to be whole and complete, to have nothing broken, nothing missing and everything going well for you. It is to have peace – the peace that passes understanding,[1] for that peace comes as a result of having perfect trust in Me and My word.[2]

AUTHOR *What do You mean by, 'not walking in the counsel of the ungodly'?*

JESUS The ungodly are those who do not focus their attention on Me. They have their own agendas, their own priorities and their own thoughts. They give no consideration to My word or to what I want or to what I say. Their plans and purposes are not Mine and they do not think as I think, or see things as I see them. If you consult with them and take notice of them they will lead you far from Me.

AUTHOR *What about standing in the path of sinners?*

JESUS There is a way that seems right to a man but in it lies destruction.[3] If you place yourself in the path of sinners then you are putting yourself in a position where they can influence you; but their ways are not Mine and their thoughts are not Mine. If you are wise then you will stay away from them. That is, you will not walk with them or go down the same path that they are treading, for their path leads to destruction.[4] I am not saying that you shouldn't stand in their path so that you can speak to them and tell them that they are going the wrong way. Clearly you must do this or else they will not know. But I am saying that you should not seek to walk with them. That is, you should not seek to do the same things or to have the same goals and purposes. Your ways are My ways. Stand in their path at the cross roads and say to them, 'You are going the wrong way. This is the way, walk in this way', for I shall direct their paths and lead them in the way they should go, if they will repent and turn from their wicked ways and follow Me. You are to be the signpost in their path showing them the correct way to go. Whether or not they listen to you is a matter for them.

AUTHOR *What about sitting in the seat of the scornful?*

JESUS Many who lack understanding are scornful. They do not understand and therefore they mock. You who have understanding should not sit with them to join them. Do not join in their conversation. Do not listen to their conversation or give it credence, for to do so will pull you down to their level and destroy you. Let your conversation and conduct be holy and pure.[5] Guard your eyes and ears against that which is contrary to My word. Protect yourself and be wise. Do not join them or listen to them. Instead, spend your time with Me and listen to Me for I have the words of eternal life.[6]

Psalm 1:2

AUTHOR *What does it mean for the blessed man to delight in Your law?*

JESUS My law is My word. If you delight in My word then you will be blessed. To delight in My word means to have pleasure in reading My word. It means to have a desire to hear what I have to say. It means that you would rather spend time finding out My mind on things rather than the world's. If you delight in My word then you will spend time reading it and listening to what I say, for I can direct you through My word and lead you in the way you should go. My word is a lamp unto your feet and a light to your path.[7] It will direct you in all things and give you wisdom and understanding. Read My word, seek My mind on things and you will indeed be blessed.

AUTHOR *What about meditating on it day and night?*

JESUS Let My word consume you and let you consume My word. Read it. Think about what I say. Do what you are doing now. Chew it over and digest it. Ask Me to explain it to you, for this is the work of the Holy Spirit to be your teacher and to give you revelation.[8] Remember that it is on revelation that I build My church.[9] There can be no true knowledge or understanding without revelation. So spend time studying and reading My word but ask the Spirit to give you understanding. As you meditate on My word and get understanding so you will be blessed and you will be a blessing to others as you share with them what I will show you.

Psalm 1:3

AUTHOR *What does it mean for him to be like a tree planted by the rivers of water?*

JESUS The rivers of water are the Holy Spirit.[10] That river of life flows out from My throne.[11] The man who meditates My word is like a tree planted by that river. That is, he is stable and sure and unshakeable. You see, there are many of My people who will just jump in the river and that is fine. It is good just to flow where My river is flowing, but there can be instability in that if there is nothing else. If there are no roots and no foundation then there is no solid ground on which to stand, and the experience of the river is experience orientated only. If this is the case then when the feelings or the experience ceases there is nothing. It is easy to be carried along by the fast flowing river having the ride of your life but there is no stability in this, so ideally there needs to be both. At the same time as you are in the river flowing with what I am doing you also need to be firmly planted on the bank. Now I know that in the natural you can't have both, but we are not talking about natural things, and in the Spirit both are possible at the same time. Therefore jump in the river and flow with what I am doing[12] and enjoy the experiences I give you, but at the same time be firmly planted in My word, for My word is your stability and anchor. Obedience to My word is the solid rock on which to build your house so that it will stand when the storms come, as they surely will.[13] So meditate on My word and be planted by the river of life with your roots drawing up the water of My Spirit. That water will keep you alive and fill you even in the driest times. Be a tree, solid and dependable, planted by the river, drawing from its waters the water of life, but also be ready to go where the river goes and flow where it flows. That is, be flexible enough to be led by My Spirit as He directs your paths.

AUTHOR *Why does he bring forth fruit in its season?*

JESUS As My Spirit directs your paths He will lead you into the fruitful places. A tree planted by the water of life will be fruitful;[14] but there are seasons of fruitfulness. I have ordained specific times and seasons for you to be fruitful, and times and seasons for you to rest, and times and seasons for you to grow. There will be many times when it may seem as though you are doing nothing. Life just appears to drift by and you think, 'Where is my fruit?' But those times, the winter times, are necessary for Me to work in you so that you can produce fruit at the appointed time. There will also be times of growth as you sit under My word and allow it to build up in you. There will be times when you sit under the ministry of the Holy Spirit and again there will be no fruit. But all the time I am working in you, and at the appointed time, in due season, it will be time for you to produce fruit and you will suddenly find a change occurs and it will be time for fruitfulness. All those barren years and times have been for this purpose and time. Do not expect to be fruitful all the time. Each of you has their own pattern of seasons and there is a time to produce fruit and there is also a time to be dormant and there is a time for growth. If you study My word and allow yourselves to be led by My Spirit you will indeed produce much fruit at the set time for producing fruit.

AUTHOR *What does it mean by his leaf shall not wither?*

JESUS Even though there is a season for producing fruit and a season for being dormant the man who is planted by the rivers of water will be a man who is always alive. The dormant season as regards producing fruit will still be a season of life, for wherever the river flows it brings life.[15] So there will always be leaves on the tree. You will not have the appearance of being dead in your dormant season but you will still be in leaf.

AUTHOR *And whatever he does shall prosper?*

JESUS Whatever you do by My Spirit will prosper. If you are a man who meditates on My word day and night and is planted by the river of the Holy Spirit, then you will be a man who can hear My voice and who will know My mind. I only did what I saw My Father doing. I only said what I heard Him say.[16] In other words I was in tune with the Spirit day and night listening to what He said to Me. If you will be guided by My word and by My Spirit then everything you turn your hand to will prosper and you will have good success in all that you do, for My Spirit will lead you and guide you into doing the things the Father ordained for you to do, and you will have good success because He has pre-ordained the works that He has called you to do.[17]

Psalm 1:4

AUTHOR *Why are the ungodly like chaff which the wind drives away?*

JESUS The ungodly do not stand by the rivers of water, neither do they meditate My word. Therefore they have no foundation in their lives and neither do they have life entering into them from My Spirit. The result is that they are blown about by every wind, by every thought, by every new thing the world throws out.[18] I am talking about Christians here. There are Christians who are ungodly. They have been saved but they do not meditate My word. If they do not meditate My word how then can they know what I am saying or what I think? They can only base their lives on the knowledge of the world, and this should not be so,[19] for I have called you out of the world into My glorious kingdom which operates on entirely different principles. Christians who do not meditate My word have no idea of these principles and they are double minded and blown about by the wind. And then there are Christians who do meditate My word but are not planted by the streams of living water. It is possible to be conscientious in studying My word but still to have no life in you.[20] The life, the revelation, the relationship with Me comes from the Holy Spirit. Being planted by the streams of living water enables you to receive that life. How can I speak things to you, and reveal My heart to you, if you are not listening to My Spirit? Both these categories of believers are ungodly and carnally minded. It is necessary to have both the word and the Spirit in order to grow strong, stable and mature.

Psalm 1:5

AUTHOR *What do You mean by the ungodly not standing in the judgement?*

JESUS I am calling My people to rule and reign with Me on this earth when I return to set up My kingdom.[21] How can My people who have not studied My word and who do not know My heart judge others? They cannot. I said that those who were faithful in the small things I have given them would be put in charge of bigger things when I came back. If you have not been faithful in the matter of studying My word and being planted by the waters then how can I entrust the things of the kingdom to you? Ungodly believers, therefore, will have taken from them the little that they have and it will be given to those of My people who have been faithful.[22] They may not lose their salvation but they will have no part in ruling and reigning with Me. It is My bride who will rule with Me and My bride is made up of those believers who have followed Me wherever I go.[23] They have dedicated themselves to Me and have not flirted with the world. They have set themselves to meditate My word and have planted themselves by the river so that they drink deeply of My Spirit, and they flow with the Spirit in whatever He wants to do. I can trust My bride to assist Me in ruling when I return.

AUTHOR *What about sinners not standing in the congregation of the righteous?*

JESUS There will be a congregation of the righteous when I return. Those who are born of My Spirit will stand in that congregation. They are righteous because I have made them so, not because of anything they have done or not done. They have accepted My righteousness as a gift[24] and they have been born again.[25] Sinners, or those who trust in their own righteousness, will not stand in this congregation for their righteousness is as filthy rags.[26] You cannot make yourselves righteous in My Father's sight.[27] Only I can stand before Him in His presence, and only those who are clothed in My righteousness can stand in His presence.[28] If you trust in your own righteousness then you are ungodly for you do not know and do not understand My word. Meditate on My word, plant yourself by the river and allow the Holy Spirit to flow in you and through you and then you will understand.

Psalm 1:6

JESUS I know the way of the righteous for I have planned his way. I have directed his paths and led him in the way he should go[29] and he has heard Me and followed Me. Therefore his way is prosperous and lies in pleasant places. But the man who has not listened to Me, who does not know My voice and who is not led by the Spirit shall not be so. He has gone his own way and thought his own thoughts and has taken no account of My ways and My thoughts which are much higher than his.[30] This man is a fool for not taking account of Me and he will perish in his unrighteousness. This is not My desire for him. I do not want this to be so, but what else can I do, for I have given him a free will. That is the greatest gift I have given you –

free will – and so I must let you exercise it even if you choose destruction and the way of death. I have given you My word. I have given you My Spirit. I have given you witnesses to point you in the right direction. What more can I do? Do not be foolish My people. Turn around. Be wise and meditate My word. Let the Spirit dwell in you to lead you and guide you. I have so much for you, if only you would listen and do this. I have plans to prosper you[31] but you must make the decision to do your part and meditate My word and act upon it, and to allow the Holy Spirit to direct you and lead you. It is both by the word and by the Spirit that you shall prosper and receive all that I have for you, My people.

Psalm Two

Psalm 2:1

AUTHOR *Lord, why do the nations rage and what is the vain thing that they plot?*

JESUS The nations have always rebelled against Me and gone their own way.[1] I sent My people Israel to show them who I am and to declare to them My purpose in the earth, but even My people Israel, to whom I have revealed Myself, have rebelled against Me. The truth of it is that My creation desires to rule itself. This has been so from the very beginning. It was this desire that caused Adam to rebel against Me.[2] But the tragedy is that you do not rule yourselves, for you have in fact submitted yourselves to the control of another master. I gave you freedom to live under My direction but Satan has stolen your freedom and caused you to be slaves to death.[3] Satan knows that his time is short[4] and it is he that rages and plots a vain thing. He uses the nations who are enslaved to him to fulfil his purposes. Yes he rages for he knows that I am coming to claim My kingdom. He is endeavouring to destroy the earth and to destroy you so that I will have nothing left to inherit. But he shall not succeed for I have saved a remnant and a posterity out of his hand who will serve Me and obey Me.[5] My people are strong for they have My Spirit within them and they shall do exploits.[6] Let My people declare that they are strong,[7] for if their God is for them who can be against them.[8] So let the nations rage, those slaves of Satan, for they cannot succeed for I am almighty and all powerful. Let them plot for their plans are indeed vain. How can they stand against Me for I have already defeated their king and master.[9]

Psalm 2:2–3

AUTHOR *Lord, why do the kings and rulers of the earth set themselves against You? Why don't they want You to rule them?*

JESUS I do not know. Who indeed would want to resist Me, when all I want, all I have ever wanted, is to love My creation and to have fellowship with them. Why indeed? That is a good question. No one in their right mind would want to stand against Me. I only want to bless the people, My people whom I have created. Why indeed? There is only one explanation. It is because they have been deceived.[10] Just as Satan deceived Eve, and Adam chose to disobey Me,[11] so My people have been deceived and have chosen to disobey Me. With disobedience comes continued deception so that they believe evil is good, and good is evil[12]. The peoples of this world are now so far away from Me that they do not know right from wrong or upside down from right way up. They have turned everything over and believe that Satan is good and that I am evil. The deception is so great that they have given themselves to serve My enemy.[13] They are totally his and he rules them, causing them to fulfil his purpose, which is to set himself above My throne.[14] So the nations rage and roar and they plot a vain thing. They try to throw off My yoke that will be on their necks. But they shall not, for I am coming to set up My kingdom and they shall not withstand Me.

Psalm 2:4

AUTHOR *Lord, why do You laugh and hold them in derision?*

JESUS I, who sit in the heavens, do laugh indeed. How do they imagine for one moment that they can stand against Me who created them?[15] Am I not the all-powerful, all-present and all-knowing God? Of course I laugh. Of course I hold them in derision, for they cannot withstand Me for one moment. Have I not already defeated their god and lord, My enemy Satan? He is already thrown out of heaven.[16] He has already had his authority stripped from him, and have I not already led him captive in triumphal procession?[17] Do I not already hold the keys to his kingdom?[18] Have I not already delegated My authority over him to My church?[19] Yes I have done all these things, so how can he hope to withstand Me? I tell you that he does not, for he knows that his time is short.[20] But the people he has deceived do really believe that they can stand against Me, for they have convinced themselves that I do not exist, that I am just a figment of the imagination of those they consider to be weak and foolish.[21] But it is they who are foolish, for it is a fool who says in his heart that there is no God.[22] The evidence of My existence is all around you.[23] Open your blind eyes and see, before I come to take up My throne, for I am coming indeed. Yes, My Father sits in the heavens and laughs them to scorn. I am coming soon and none shall withstand Me.[24]

Psalm 2:5–6

JESUS Yes, My Father shall speak to them in His wrath for He has given them plenty of opportunity to repent.[25] He has sent His prophets, He has sent Me, and now He has sent the church, but they have ignored all. Yes, He is angry at what they have done. Yes, He is angry that they have joined His enemy and they have sought to destroy this world that He gave them. Yes, He is angry that they have rejected Me, His only Son, and that they have rejected and persecuted you, My beloved bride. Yes, His displeasure is deep and He declares to them that He has set Me on His holy hill of Zion to rule this earth. Enough is enough! Your time has run out, your lease on the earth is withdrawn, and I am coming to take back My kingdom and rule in person. Yes, you will see Me ruling in Jerusalem, the city of the Great King.[26] Let the nations rage and plot and plan and reject their God, but it will not be for much longer. I see what is going on in the earth. I am not blind. I know what you do and I say it is enough. I am coming. Yes I am coming very soon to sit on My holy hill of Zion.

Psalm 2:7

AUTHOR *Lord, why did Your Father declare that You were His Son and when was the day that You were begotten?*

JESUS There were two ways in which I was the Son of My Father. I was the Son of God and I was the Son of Man. As the Son of God I was My Father's Son, for as the Word of God I was begotten of the Father the moment that He spoke.[27] When you speak, your words are an expression of you and are begotten by you. When My Father spoke, His Word was an expression of Him and begotten by Him. But His Word was, and is, a living being and His Word is Spirit[28] and His Word is alive and active.[29] His Word is the expression of His power and by the Word of His power everything is sustained.[30] That Word is a living being for it is begotten of the Father who is a Spirit. I am the Word of God and I am a living being. I am a Spirit who is one with the Father and the expression of the Father. When the Word spoken by the Father was carried to Mary by the angel and she received Me,[31] I became clothed in flesh and the Word of God became a man,[32] the man JESUS, Immanuel, God with us.[33] Therefore I was the only begotten Son of the Father. No other man came into being in this way, and I Jesus am the only begotten Son of the Father. However, I died. That is, I was separated from the Father on the cross when I became sin for you.[34] Eternal life is to know the Father[35] and when I became separated from Him[36] I no longer had His Life within Me and I entered into death. This is the state that you are in when you are born. You are born into death, into separation from the Father. This is why it is necessary for you to be born again to enter into a relationship with Him so that you can know Him and have Eternal Life.[37] But I did not remain in a state of death, for My Father raised Me up. The mighty power of the Holy Spirit came to Me and joined Himself to My spirit causing My spirit to be reborn.[38] On this day, the day of My resurrection, I became the first human being to be born from above[39] and on this day the Father declared that a human being had become His Son. On this day, as a human being, I was begotten of the Father, the firstfruit,[40] the first of many human beings who would be born from above and become sons of God, for the same mighty power, the same Holy Spirit who raised Me up has raised you up also[41] and given you the power to become sons of the living God. You are new creations, a new being that has never been before.[42] You are begotten of the Father. So on this day, the day of My resurrection, your Father, and My Father, declared to the world that I, as the Son of Man, had become His Son, the first of many, and as the Son of Man I will reign from His holy hill of Zion, for the earth He has given to the sons of men. As the Son of God I rule in heaven under My Father for the heavens belong to God, but as the Son of Man I rule on the earth because the earth He has given to the children of men.[43]

Psalm 2:8

AUTHOR *Lord, why did the Father tell You to ask for the nations for Your inheritance?*

JESUS It is the Father's desire that all men should know Him and have a relationship with Him.[44] Did He not walk and talk with Adam in the garden? You do not understand the distress He was in when Adam hid from Him. 'Adam, where are you?' was a cry that echoed round the garden[45] and it is a cry that has echoed down the ages. 'Adam, where are you?' reverberates around the universe as your Father seeks you in His distress. He longs and yearns for that fellowship to be restored, for that is why He created you. And that is why He sent Me, so that it can be restored. When you cry, 'Father, I am here. I'm sorry, I repent', He comes running to you. Did I not give you a picture of your Father in the parable of the prodigal son.[46] That picture is a picture more of the Father than of the son. So yes, your Father wants all men to come to Him to be saved. He does not want any to be lost and so He sent Me, and for My inheritance He has promised to give Me the nations – all those who will return to Him, who will come running to Him in repentance.

AUTHOR *Lord, why do You have to ask Him for the nations when He has promised them to You?*

JESUS Your Father has given the earth to the children of men. This is your domain, your sphere of authority. He will not intervene or interfere unless you ask Him. Therefore as a child of men I have to ask Him to give Me the nations as My inheritance, and I have done that as your King. Many people will be in My kingdom and many will be restored to fellowship with their Father. Once again He will be able to walk the earth in the cool of the evening and fellowship with His creation. That cry of, 'Adam, where are you?' will no longer be a cry of despair and of great loss, for now you will answer, 'I'm here Father. Let us walk together'. No longer will the sons of men hide from His presence in fear of what they have done, but they will come running, as little children run to their daddy in delight when he comes home. Yes, My Father and your Father has come home to you. He will make His dwelling with you[47] and He will delight in My inheritance, His children, once again.

Psalm 2:9

AUTHOR *Lord, when You receive the nations as Your inheritance why will You break them with a rod of iron and dash them in pieces like a potter's vessel?*

JESUS When I return the whole earth will belong to Me, but not all will submit to Me. Although My Father longs for the nations to turn to Him there are many who will still oppose Him. Many are the sons of His enemy Satan, and like their father[48] they wish to exalt themselves above God.[49] They will oppose Him right to the end. Well, enough is enough. When I return I am not going to permit this to go on any longer. All those who stand against Me, all those who oppose Me, I will destroy.[50] The age of grace will be closed and the day of vengeance will be here. It has gone on long enough. We have given you more than enough opportunity to repent. For the sake of those who do want My rule, I will crush and destroy those who want My enemy Satan to rule instead. No more. I say no more. It is time. Many ask, 'why doesn't God do something about the state of the world?' Well, it is time. I have delayed long enough. I only delayed to give more people time to return to Me[51] but now it is time to wind this up. The age of grace will be closed and it is time for the completion of all things.[52] I will only be rejected for so long and when I return it will be to impose My rule and My will on this world as your King, the Son of Man. I will indeed crush all opposition for I am determined to hand the kingdom to My Father so that He can enjoy fellowship with His children, those who are called by His name and who long for His presence.

Psalm 2:10–11

FATHER Therefore now is the time to be wise. Now is the time to be instructed. My word is available to all of you. I have given you the written word so that you will know, so that you will have knowledge, so that you will have understanding.[53] Is this not enough for you, My people? I have set forth My word and I have laid bare My heart to you. I have shown you that from the beginning of time My desire has been for all of you to come to a knowledge of Me.[54] I have set forth My way. I have set forth My standards. I have set forth My judgements and I have called you to order. Not only have I set before you My law to show you what I require of you, but I have sent forth My Spirit to create in you a new heart and a clean heart that will give you the desire to obey Me. I have made it possible for you to keep My statutes, for I have offered to place My Spirit within you to give you both the desire and the ability to keep My word.[55] I do not ask of you too hard a thing. I do not ask of you the impossible, for I have made provision for your weakness and your inability to obey Me. No, indeed I have come Myself, by My

Spirit, to live in you both to will and to do of My good pleasure.[56] Is it too great a thing for Me to expect you to co-operate with Me in this, when I have done all that is necessary on your behalf to bring you salvation? I do not want to pass judgement upon you to bring you to destruction, but I must do this if you reject Me and what I have done for you. You leave Me no choice if you continue in your rebellious and wicked ways. So My people, you kings and judges, you leaders of this world, turn aside from your own ways and your own understanding and seek counsel of Me,[57] says the Lord your God. I have given you My word. I have given you the truth. I have given you the way, in written form, and I advise you to seek instruction and to seek wisdom from Me before it is too late. But note this you people, I have not dealt unfairly with you, for not only have I given you My written word but I have also sent My living Word, My Son, to live among you and to demonstrate to you what I require. I have not only told you the way in My written word but I have sent My Word to be the Way, to be the Truth and to be the Life.[58] You cannot come to Me except by Him, for I have provided no other way for you to be saved.[59] So be wise and be instructed you people of the earth. Come to My Son and worship Him. Honour Him, obey Him, for He is your Way, He is your Word, He is your Life. Serve Him with fear. Understand who He is and rejoice with trembling in all that He has done for you.

Psalm 2:12

AUTHOR *Lord, why should we kiss the Son?*

FATHER My Son is your liege Lord. He is your rightful King that I have set before you. Pay homage to Him. Kiss His hand in an act of fealty. Swear to Him that you accept Him as your Lord and King and then He will not be angry.[60] He is not angry with you for He loves you and He died for you. He desires you for His bride. You are His very great reward for all that He suffered on your behalf.[61] But just as My Son bowed His knee to Me to accomplish this, so must you bow your knee to Him. Because He submitted and subordinated His own will to Mine, so now I have highly exalted Him and given Him a name that is above every other name, and I tell you now, that at the name of Jesus every knee will bow and every tongue will confess that He is Lord and My King.[62] Every being in heaven and on earth, and indeed under the earth, will kiss the Son or My very great anger will be aroused against them. You do not want to be the subject of My wrath for who can stand against My righteous anger.[63] So kiss the Son now, voluntarily while you can, and do not be forced to bow the knee to Him in His anger. For if you wait until then you will indeed perish in the way. Now is the day of salvation.[64] Bow the knee now, out of your own free will, whilst it is still the age of grace and My grace and My blessing can abound towards you. Do it now. Submit to Him now out of your own free will, for many are the blessings that will chase after those who choose Him as their King now.[65] His wrath is kindled but a little at this time, but soon His wrath will be seen in full force when He comes to claim His throne.[66] Do not delay. Do not wait until then, I implore you. Kiss the Son now. Choose Him now to be your Lord and I will pour out on you so much blessing that you will not be able to contain it.[67] I have so much to give you that you cannot even conceive of,[68] so kiss the Son now, pay homage to Him now, and swear fealty to Him now while you can still choose to do so. But do not be deceived, the day is shortly and surely coming when I will install My King in Zion and He will rule this earth with a rod of iron. Come, rule with Him.[69] Do not be crushed by Him.[70] Come, choose Him now, for He is indeed coming to claim His inheritance very soon.

AUTHOR *Lord, what does it mean for us to put our trust in the Son?*

FATHER My Son is the one that I have sent to you to give you access into My kingdom.[71] You cannot come into My presence, you cannot enter into My kingdom trusting in your own righteousness, for your righteousness is as filthy rags in My sight.[72] No, put your trust in Him for He paid for your sin and He gave you His righteousness.[73] Come to Me in His righteousness, not your own. He is everything to you. He is the way that you can come to Me. He is the life that you will live in My presence and He is the truth of My word that I have spoken to you. Only in Him can you be reunited with Me, for I am holy. I am a consuming fire[74] and a burning oven[75] that will destroy you if you approach Me trusting in your own deeds, in your own works, and in your own righteousness.[76] Do you not understand that you are wicked and evil, that there is nothing good in you. You are totally depraved and desperately wicked and there is no remedy.[77] There is nothing that can make you holy and acceptable to Me, that will allow you to enter into My presence without being destroyed by My holy fire. No, there is no remedy. You cannot under any circumstances make yourself acceptable to Me by what you do or by what you say. So stop trying! Stop being religious, for no religion can make you holy. You are totally and irrevocably evil and must be destroyed.[78] Is there, then, no hope for you? Yes there is! There is a hope, and My Son is your hope.[79] What is the answer then? The answer is that you must die, for the wages of your sin is death and there is no escaping that. But if you will die voluntarily and put your trust in My Son then He will raise you up again[80] and your life will be hid in Him.[81] It will not be you who lives but He who lives in you,[82] and you will come to Me, not trusting in your own righteous deeds but in His, and because you will be hidden in Him you will be holy and acceptable to Me. What do you have to do to trust in My Son? Just call on His name.[83] Accept that you can do nothing for yourself and call on Him to save you.[84] Bow the knee to Him now. Declare Him to be your King now. Submit your will to His now and ask Him to save you, and He will. It is not too difficult a thing for Him to accomplish.[85] Kiss the Son now, for blessed are all those who put their trust in Him, for they shall see My face and they shall abide in My glorious presence for ever.[86] This the cry of the heart of the Father. I love you My child and I want you to be with Me. Come to Jesus now so that you can come into My presence and be with Me forever,[87] and make the heart of your Father glad indeed.[88]

Psalm Three

Psalm 3:1–2

AUTHOR *Lord, there is much increase of trouble in the world and many of Your people are being affected by national events and are suffering on a personal level. The world says, 'Where is your God?' Will You encourage us?*

JESUS Did I not say that these times would come? Did I not say that persecutions, trials and tribulations would come in the last days?[1] When you see these things beginning to happen then look up and rejoice for your salvation is drawing near.[2] These are the birth pangs of the new age of My kingdom.[3] Before I come My kingdom must be born, and it will be born in much travail. Out of the distress of these times will come a glorious time. So do not be downhearted My people, do not be despondent for trials and tribulations must come. I told you this before I left. If they persecuted Me then they will persecute you.[4] You are not immune from the tribulation that is in the world for you live in the world,[5] but you are immune from the judgement that will come on the earth, for you shall not be judged for you have already passed from death to life and into

My kingdom.[6] Therefore what should your attitude be amongst trials and tribulations, when it seems that everything and everyone is against you?[7] Rejoice, rejoice, rejoice,[8] for you have a hope and a future![9] I will not leave you desolate. I am with you always, and through everything and in everything.[10] Rejoice, My people, in all circumstances for that is My will for you.[11] Keep your eyes fixed on Me who am the author and the finisher of your faith.[12] I am the beginning of your faith and I am the end of your faith.[13] In Me you shall overcome, and I have much blessing for those who overcome.[14] Give thanks, for I have overcome the world. Do not fret because of evil doers.[15] Do not be upset because the enemy comes against you like a flood. Turn your eyes to Me and I will raise up the standard of My Spirit against him on your behalf.[16] Stand still, stand firm, and watch, and I will part the red sea for you.[17] I will make a way when there seems that there is no way. I have not forgotten you. Do not listen to the voice of your enemy. I will never forget you, for how could a mother forget her child?[18] You are My children and you are very precious to Me. I will fight for you, for the battle belongs to Me. It is not yours.[19] Stand firm, keep your eyes fixed on Me and I will deliver you from your enemies. Do not look at the circumstances; do not look at what is going on in the world. Do not look at the storms that come against you. No, look to Me and I will save you. When Peter walked on the water he took his eyes off Me, and looked instead at the wind and the waves, and he began to sink.[20] What have wind and waves and storms to do with walking on the water? Nothing. It wasn't the wind and the waves that caused him to sink. It was taking his eyes off Me. So keep your eyes fixed on Me in the midst of the storms of life and in the midst of trouble and persecution. When it seems that the enemy is coming against you like a flood keep your eyes on Me. Reach out to Me in all your distress and I will save you. Believe Me, that there is help indeed for you in Me, whatever your enemy might say.

Psalm 3:3

AUTHOR *Lord, what does it mean for You to be a shield for me?*

FATHER I am your strong tower and a fortress around you. If you run into Me you will be safe.[21] I mean that if you stay close to Me, if you stay close to My word and obedient to My word then I can protect you. We have entered into a covenant, you and I, when you made Jesus your Lord.[22] Because you have made Me your God[23] I am duty bound by this covenant, that I have initiated, to protect you. As your God I am your shield and your strong defender.[24] If any person or any principality or power attacks you then they will have to deal with Me, your covenant partner.[25] When you were little you would stand behind your daddy. He would stand between you and any danger. Have you not heard children say when threatened, 'I will get my dad onto you,' for their dad is bigger than they are. Well, I am your Dad and I am bigger than anyone. Just as you would cling to your daddy and hide behind him peering round his legs, so you can hide behind Me and I will protect you. I am your shield and a very present help in time of trouble.[26] So when you are threatened or distressed by any enemy, whether circumstances, storms of life, human beings, or principalities, powers and demons, remember that I am there for you and you can hide behind Me, and if I am for you who can be against you.[27] I am your strong tower, your fortress and your protection and if you will run to Me in your trouble I can help you. As your covenant partner I have obligated Myself to do this, therefore you must uphold your part in the covenant, which is to obey My word and abide in My presence.[28] If you will do this then no-one can touch you.

AUTHOR *What does it mean for You to be my glory and the One who lifts up my head?*

FATHER I am the One who justifies you. You do not need to justify yourself before your enemies. When your enemies say all manner of evil things against you falsely for My name's sake[29] then do not try to justify yourself, for I am the One who will establish your righteousness in the face of your enemies.[30] Remember Jesus. He did not say anything before His accusers to justify Himself or who He was. He remained silent and trusted Me to vindicate Him.[31] And I did, did I not? I raised Him up, glorified Him and sat Him down at My right hand[32] so that all the world will know that He is My Son.[33] And I will do the same for you if you have His attitude. If you will remain humble and not try to justify yourself then I will raise you up.[34] I will declare your righteousness, I will vindicate you in the assembly, for vengeance is Mine and I will repay.[35] Trust Me and I will lift up your head and give you honour before your enemies.[36]

Psalm 3:4

AUTHOR *Lord, sometimes it doesn't seem as though You hear us when we cry to You.*

FATHER My child, I always hear you. I listen for your voice all the time. My ear is strained to hear you. You do not utter one sound but I hear you. You do not make one movement but I see you. You do not think one thought that I am not aware of. I am acutely aware of everything you do, say or think, because you are so special to Me and I love you so much.[37] Do not think that I ignore your cries. I am not like some of you who have been taught to ignore your baby's cries. I am there for you the moment you utter a sound. I pick you up, I cuddle you, I comfort you and I love you. Underneath you are the everlasting arms[38] and I will never let you go.[39] I will never ignore you. Now, I know that sometimes you do not feel as though I am there, but I am nevertheless. Remember that you walk by faith and not by sight.[40] Your senses are deceptive. Do not rely on them. Rely on My word, for My word is sure.[41] My word is a solid rock and you can trust it. I have said that I am there for you, I have said that I hear you, I have said that I answer you, I have said that I will comfort you, I have said that I will protect you, I have said that I will never forsake you and that under you are the everlasting arms. If I have said it, then it is so, whether you feel it or not. My word is sure. I do not lie.[42] Trust Me. I do hear you when you cry to Me and I do answer you. Believe My word, not your feelings. Learn to walk by faith and not by sight for then you will not be dismayed when your senses fail to react to Me, for I operate in the Spirit and not in the flesh.

Psalm 3:5

FATHER My child you can sleep peacefully. I give My children rest.[43] In the midst of the storm you can sleep peacefully. Did not Jesus sleep in the midst of a storm?[44] That was because He had perfect trust in Me. He had no fear for He knew that the storm could not touch Him, because His times were in My hands.[45] And I will protect you in like manner if you will put your trust in Me as He did. The disciples were amazed that He could sleep when they thought they were about to die, and people of the world will be amazed also when they see how calm you are in the midst of the storms of life. Your peace in these circumstances will pass all their understanding[46] and they will marvel and they will question. Then you will be able to tell them[47] that your peace comes from having a perfect trust in your Father. And that trust in Me comes from knowing Me, knowing who I am, and knowing what I am like, and knowing that My love for you is perfect.[48] So yes you can lie down and sleep and leave your enemies to Me, confident that I will look after you and protect you and that you will awake refreshed and ready for the fray. For I will give you refreshing sleep and I will sustain you and fill you and strengthen you as you abide quietly in My presence.

Psalm 3:6

FATHER You need not be afraid My son if I am for you. It does not matter how many come against you. It does not matter how bad things seem. It does not matter if the whole world comes against you for I am greater than the world. I am greater than any of your enemies. I am greater than all of them put together, so even if Satan and all his forces are arrayed against you, you need have no fear for I am greater than them all. Do not be afraid for I am with you. You can hide behind your Daddy's legs and scoff at your enemies for I am your shield and your strong defender. No one can get to you without My permission, and I love you and I have your best interests at heart. So fear not, fear not, fear not. Greater is He who is in you than he who is in the world.[49] Fear not, fear not, fear not, for if I am for you who can be against you?[50] Remember Elisha when he was surrounded by the Syrian army, how he prayed for his servant's eyes to be opened and he saw the mountains full of horses and chariots of fire.[51] Pray that your eyes too will be opened and you too will see the angels that I have assigned to protect you.[52] No My son, even if tens of thousands set themselves against you they cannot prosper in their evil designs, for the host of heaven is surrounding you to protect you. Open your eyes and see and believe, and you will sleep soundly with no fear and with great peace in your heart.

Psalm 3:7

AUTHOR *Lord, what does it mean for You to have struck my enemies on the cheekbone and broken the teeth of the ungodly?*

FATHER Every tongue that rises against you in judgement you shall condemn, for this is your heritage in Me, says your Lord.[53] No weapon that is formed against you can prosper, and nor shall it, for I have defeated your enemies. I have destroyed their ability to devour you for I have broken their jaw and their cheekbone. Your enemy Satan is a toothless lion looking for those who out of ignorance will allow him to destroy them.[54] He cannot harm you unless you let him. His power and his authority is broken. His words can no longer harm you. Indeed you shall resist him by the words that come from your mouth. Let your words be My words,[55] and you will have great power over your enemy as you speak, according to the words that I shall give you, in the power of My Spirit. In your tongue you have the ability and the power to condemn your enemy,[56] as you speak according to My word, for I have given you authority to use My name as My attorney on the earth.[57] Do not allow your enemy to fool you and ride roughshod over you. Lift up your voice and speak My words as I give you utterance by My Spirit and you will see your enemy flee before you as you declare, 'It is written'.[58] This is your heritage as My son and My heir.[59] Use your inheritance. You do not need to call on Me to save you for I have given you the victory[60] and I have given you the weapons to enforce that victory, so hold up your shield of faith, place your helmet of salvation on your head, gird your waist with truth, wear your breastplate of righteousness and walk with the gospel of peace on your feet, with your two edged sword, My word, coming out of your mouth.[61] The victory is already yours. Walk in it, exercise it, claim it, enforce it, for I am with you to back you with My name in all that My Spirit leads you to do and say.

Psalm 3:8

FATHER Salvation belongs to Me and your righteousness is of Me, says the Lord your God and your Father.[62] You have My blessing so stand up and take the land,[63] take your inheritance, for I have given it to you.[64] Stand firm against those who would oppose you, who would rise up against you and seek to cheat you out of your blessing. Do not be afraid if trouble increases. Do not be afraid if many rise up against you for I am with you indeed, and I will support you and protect you with all that I have and with all that I am. I have given you My name.

Psalm Eight

Psalm 8:1

AUTHOR *Lord, talk to me about the excellence of Your name in all the earth.*

JESUS My name is above every other name.[1] There is no name like My name in the whole of creation. My name is a name that will be recognised throughout this earth. At present My name is not known throughout the earth. Indeed the excellence of My name is not even known throughout much of what calls itself My church. Many of My people have no understanding of what My name means or what it represents. They do not understand the power and the authority that is in My name. They have no concept of what it means to be given the privilege of using My name. At My name every knee shall bow and every tongue confess that I am Lord. My church needs a revelation of what is embodied in My name and what authority they have when they invoke My name.[2] My name will open doors for them that would otherwise be closed. My name opens the way into the very throne room of the Father. If they understood the esteem in which all of heaven holds My name, they would come boldly into the throne room of grace and ask what they will of the Father, and He would give them all that they desire.[3] My people must get a revelation of the authority and power that they hold in My name. The enemy trembles at My name. No principality or power can withstand My name. Wake up My church and understand your inheritance in the name that I have given to you.[4] Take My name throughout this earth and bring glory to the Father. Make My name known to the heathen. Tell of what I have done and what I am. Tell of what I have done for you. Tell how My name has impacted your life.[5] Make My name known throughout all the earth and to the ends of the world. My name shall indeed be excellent in all the earth.

AUTHOR *Lord, what does it mean by, 'You who have set Your glory above the heavens'?*

FATHER My glory is established in the heavens. The weight of My presence is known throughout heaven. It is established and permanent. My glory rests heavily in My throne room.[6] My glory is established above the earth in the realm in which I dwell. Moses wanted to see My glory and I allowed My goodness to pass before him so that he saw My back side.[7] You cannot see My glory and live, in your present bodies. Do not ask to see My glory, for if you do see it you will be instantly destroyed. Rather ask to see manifestations of My presence and I will reveal a little of Myself to you, for I do not want you to be destroyed. The day will come when My glory will be seen by you,[8] but not now, not in this age. I will reveal to you what I can of My presence and that will more than satisfy you. Do not seek to see My glory for you cannot. You do not know for what you ask. My glory I have set above the heavens, to protect you, and there it shall remain for now, until the time appointed for My presence to dwell with you on the earth.[9]

Psalm 8:2

AUTHOR *Father, why have You ordained strength out of the mouth of babes and infants?*

FATHER Children know how to praise Me and worship Me without hindrance. You adults have become too sophisticated. This is why Jesus said that you must become like little children to enter the kingdom of heaven.[10] You must become as children because I am your Father, and the relationship that I want to have with you is that of parent and child. Young children accept what their parents say. There is a simple trust between a child and his father. When the child grows up and becomes a teenager the child is influenced by all sorts of other people and things, and no longer readily accepts the wisdom of his parents. You have become as teenagers, questioning My wisdom and thinking that you know better than Me. How could you know better than Me? How could you have more wisdom than I, for I created you? I want you to become as little children again. I want you to return to the age of innocence when you had perfect trust in the wisdom and ability of your father. Do you remember the time when you thought that your father was perfect and he knew everything and could do anything? This is how I want you to be with Me, for I do know everything, I can do anything and nothing is too difficult for Me.[11] Return to being Daddy's child and put your trust in Me. Jesus said that out of the mouths of babes and sucklings I have perfected praise.[12] True praise comes when you accept Me for who I am, when you take My word at face value and when you put your little hand in My big hand and walk securely with Me. Then you can gaze up at Me, your Daddy, in awe and wonder, and then your praise and your worship will be perfect indeed and in this will be your strength.

AUTHOR *Father, what does this have to do with Your enemies and enabling You to silence the enemy and the avenger?*

FATHER My enemy is Satan, the adversary[13] and the avenger. He is My enemy because he attacks you, My children. He works by deceit, telling lies about Me.[14] He misrepresents Me to My children[15] and I hate him. He deceives My people and when they believe the lie he can gain the victory over them. O My children, if you will be as little children, if you will believe My word and put your trust in Me instead of the lie, I can keep you safe. If you will praise Me and worship Me then in that will be your strength. As you praise Me and worship Me, your Father, Satan can have no hold over you. He only gains control over you because you believe his lie. When you praise Me and worship Me, indicating that you have put your trust in Me, I can turn to My enemy and still his voice for he cannot have victory over you whilst you are believing and trusting in Me. Give thanks to Me, give praise to Me, in all circumstances,[16] and you will not open the door of your mind to his deceits and lies.[17] As you become My little children again, having perfect trust in Me, your praise and your worship will be your strength and I can still the enemy and the avenger on your behalf. He was only able to deceive Eve because she did not fully trust Me. He sowed seeds of doubt into her mind and she began to reason that I was holding out on her.[18] If she had had perfect trust in Me as her Daddy she would not have opened the door of her mind to his lies. Perfect love casts out fear.[19] The enemy sowed fear and doubt and unbelief. Do not allow him to do this to you.[20] I love you perfectly as My child. I will not withhold anything good from you for I love you with an everlasting and perfect love.[21] If you love and trust Me, if you believe that I love you perfectly, then there can be no room for fear and doubt to enter your mind. Perfect love, perfect trust, as a little child has for her wonderful daddy, casts out all fear. In daddy's presence all is well and nothing can go wrong. In daddy's presence there is no fear. I am your perfect Daddy. Believe that I love you and care for you, and out of your mouth will come praise, and that praise will be your strength against the enemy and the avenger, that father of all lies who is Satan.[22]

Psalm 8:3

AUTHOR *Father, talk to me about the works of Your fingers.*

FATHER I have created the heavens, I have created the moon and the stars, just for you. I am an extravagant God and I have created everything just for you. Nothing is too much, for you My precious son. Everything that you see, everything that you touch, everything that you smell, taste and hear; everything is for you. I created the earth in all its intricate and wondrous detail just for you, just for your pleasure and your delight. I did not create it for Me for I have My own realm. No, the earth and all that is in it, all its fullness and glory and wonder, I created just to delight you and to show you how much I love you. Nothing is too much trouble for Me where you are concerned. You are My child and I adore you. I wanted you to understand My nature, that I am generous beyond compare. I have created stars and stars and stars, millions and millions of them, just for you. Why did I create such an extravagant number? Just to show you My nature, that I am an extravagant God. Just to make you wonder. Just to make you stand in awe and know that I am God. And I did all that just for you. But not just the stars; look around you. What do you see? Look at all the animals, the fish, the birds, the plants. Look at the amazing variety of shapes and sizes. Look at all the different colours. Look around you and see the precision of My creation. Look around you. You will never fathom it. You will never get to the bottom of it. You will never work it all out. You will never run out of things to explore. You have hardly touched the surface with all your knowledge and understanding. There is so much, so much, too much, more than you could ever want or need. There is always something more for you to find out. Look at My creation. It is so intricate, so delicate, so finely balanced and tuned. How can you say there is no God and that it just happened by chance? No, you cannot say that, for it shrieks of Me. It cries out about Me. My creation tells you about Me, your loving Father.[23]

Stand in awe and wonder, gaze and wonder how it all fits together, but remember that all of this, every bit of it, every detail, I have created just for you. I didn't create it for Me. I created it for you. Just for you. There is no point to the creation if you are not here to share it with. I long to share it with you, to share its secrets, to give you revelation and understanding, if only you would come to Me. But you have corrupted your ways. You have denied Me and gone your own way, and I am grieved. Come back to Me and let Me share My creation with you. Let Me show you its secrets, for I delight in revealing them to you, for I am your Father and I delight in you, My precious child. And all this, every bit of it, I made just for you.

Psalm 8:4–5

AUTHOR *Lord, what is man that You are mindful of him?*

FATHER What is man? Man is My creation. Man is the pinnacle and the height of My creation. But more than that, much, much more than that, man is My son, My daughter, born of My Spirit, My own Spirit, My own offspring.[24] Oh you do not understand who and what you are. Do you not realise that you are created in My image.[25] Just stop and think about that for a minute. Who am I? What am I like? I am the Supreme Being, the Self-existent and Eternal One, and you are like Me. I created you to be like Me. No you are not self-existent and eternal in yourselves, but you are eternal in Me for you have My life within you. When I created you, you were perfect just like Me. You have the same kind of mind that I have, you think, talk and feel in the same way that I do. You have the same desire and drive to rule and create that I have. I created you to be just like Me so that I could have fellowship with you, so that I could walk and talk with you, and so that we could understand each other.[26] But you spoiled all that and became corrupted. However, I have rescued you and reinstated you. Indeed I have gone further than before, for you are no longer just My creation but now you are My sons and My daughters. No other being, however glorious, can match you in your recreated state, for no other being is created in My image.[27] The angels are in awe of you for they understand who you are, even if you do not. They count it a great privilege to serve Me by serving you.[28] They know that next to Me you are the highest being in existence for I created you only a little lower than Myself.[29] Do not despise yourselves for you are glorious beings and I created the whole of the natural universe just for you to look after and govern. I have done that for no other being. I want you to understand who you are, for you have too lowly a picture of yourselves. You consider yourselves to be a no-man and a worm,[30] but you are not. I made Jesus to be that for you,[31] so that you could be raised up in Him to sit with Me in heavenly places.[32] What are you that I should visit you and be mindful of you? You are the supremacy of My creation and only I am higher than you. Take a look at Jesus, at the picture of Jesus in Revelation chapter one.[33] You see Him as the glorified Christ shining brighter than the noonday sun, and John fell at His feet in dread.[34] But, but, but, My children, John was still in the flesh when He saw Jesus. John was still wearing the veil of the flesh. When Jesus comes you will be like Him.[35] You will be revealed to the whole of creation and they will see you as you truly are[36] You will be like Jesus in His glorified state for you are His bride. That picture of Jesus is also a picture of you, for you are in Him. He is the firstborn among many brethren.[37] Yes He is your Lord and your creator, but He is also your brother. If you want to know why I am mindful of you then think of why I am mindful of Him, for you are just like Him. Once the veil of your flesh is removed, the whole of creation will see you as you truly are, its lord and master. What is man that I am mindful of him? Man is My offspring, spirit of My Spirit.[38] That is why I am mindful of you, because you are My child and I am your Father. This is why I am mindful of you, because I love you. I love you. I love you so much, My precious, precious, child. I have crowned you with glory and honour, just as I have crowned Jesus, for you and He are one. Indeed you and I are one, for Jesus prayed that this would be so, and I have answered His prayer indeed.[39]

Psalm 8:6–8

AUTHOR *Father, why did You make us to have dominion over the works of Your hands and put all things under our feet?*

FATHER My son, as I have already explained to you, I have created you in My image and to be My son. It is in My nature to create and to rule, and to have dominion, and therefore it is in yours also. I want you to be like Me for you are My child, so I have created for you a realm of your own. The heavens belong to

Me but the earth I have given to you.[40] Even though I knew that Adam would rebel I gave him the greatest gift of all, the gift of free will. I needed to do this for, as I have said, I wanted sons who are like Me. I have free will and therefore you also must have free will. But of course, in giving you a free will and a place in which to exercise that will, there was always the possibility, indeed the certainty, that you would make wrong choices. But I had a plan, before the earth was founded, that would come against that, and would overcome that and restore you to fellowship with Me.[41] And that I have done and am doing. So, I gave you a place of your own that you could run on My behalf and that I could share with you. I gave you an animal kingdom to look after and care for, as I care for you, and I gave you the ability to have children of your own to fellowship with.[42] But you have abused what I gave you and are destroying it. You have not had the wisdom that I initially gave you for you bowed the knee to My enemy Satan. However the time is coming when one of you will rule over this creation in justice and in wisdom.[43] He is the man Jesus. Although He is My Son, the Son of God, He is also the Son of man, and as the Son of man He will lead you and direct you.[44] He will restore all things and hand them back to Me.[45] I will renew the earth and the heavens that I gave you.[46] I will recreate them so that once again they will be perfect and I will give them back to you as your inheritance as My sons.[47] Only this time there will be no enemy to spoil things, to come between us, and I will fulfil My original purpose which was to have sons that I could enjoy, have fellowship with and live with.[48] In that day you will fully appreciate what I have given you, what a wonderful creation this earth is, how beautiful it is and how glorious. All will be in harmony. There will be no death or destruction and you My people, My children, will inherit it and rule it for Me with love and with wisdom. And I shall visit you, indeed I will come and live with you, and we shall have fellowship together for ever more. So, My children, this is why I have given you dominion on the earth, for it is yours. I made it for you and I know that you will one day truly appreciate My gift to you and know how much I love you and want to be with you.

Psalm 8:9

AUTHOR *Oh Lord, our Lord, how excellent is Your name in all the earth.*

FATHER Yes, in that day My name will be known by all, for all will know Me. The earth and the heavens will know Me for who I am, and the knowledge of Me will be throughout the earth.[49] And you, My children, will have access to My knowledge and wisdom and you will rule wisely My creation. Heaven and earth in that day will be united and there will be no barrier between them. My name will indeed be excellent and known throughout the earth.

Psalm Fourteen

Psalm 14:1

AUTHOR *Lord, why is the person who says that there is no God a fool? What is a fool?*

FATHER A fool is someone who is either stupid or wicked. A wicked man is one who understands that what he is doing is contrary to My word. He is a person who has made a choice to subject himself to the kingdom of darkness and to My enemy Satan. The purpose of his heart is to do wickedly continually.[1] He has no other thought or purpose than to gratify his own desires and wishes, and My enemy Satan will give him every opportunity to do just that. This man has no pleasure in righteousness[2] and he has made himself his own god, or even worse, he has chosen Satan as his god and deliberately chooses to serve him through witchcraft or other occult practices. This man is a fool because he believes that Satan can win against Me. This man is a fool because he chooses to ignore the fact that I exist, so that he can gratify his own desires. This man is a fool because he chooses to believe that he can sow without reaping and that there will be no consequences to his actions.[3]

A stupid man is one who, although not deliberately seeking to do evil, chooses to ignore the evidence of My existence. He is so self conscious that he cannot be God conscious. Again this man has made himself to be his own god. He exalts his own intellect above that of his Creator.[4] He exalts his own ideas, his own desires and his own purposes above Mine. He makes himself his own god and serves only his own feeble ideas.[5] Both the stupid man and the wicked man are fools for they both ignore Me, their Creator, and assume that there will be no consequences following on from their stupidity.[6] A man who says in his heart that there is no God is a fool for I have given ample evidence of My existence. I have not left you without proof that I exist,[7] for I have placed within each of you an understanding and a knowledge of Me, but the fool chooses to ignore this.

I have given you the evidence of My creation. My creation screams at you that there is a creator.[8] How can you possibly believe that this creation happened by chance? It is so finely balanced, so finely tuned, that no one in their right mind could believe it just came together by accident. How many of you have seen an explosion that creates order? A big bang creates disorder. Since when have you seen an explosion result in a finely tuned and balanced order? My people, it takes more faith to believe that this world came about by accident than it does to believe that I made it. I have given you ample proof of My existence in My creation. But I have given you more than that. I have given you witnesses, thousands and thousands of witnesses down the ages who will all testify of Me.[9] How many witnesses do you need to prove a case in court? I have given you thousands, so do not say that there is no evidence for My existence. It is indeed a fool who says in his heart that there is no God. And finally I came Myself, as the Man Jesus, to testify to you of Me, through what He said and what He did.[10] He testified of Me in His death and in His resurrection, and He continues to testify of Me in the changed lives of countless millions who are daily putting their trust in Me. Do not be a fool My people. Know that I AM,[11] and that I am the Alpha and the Omega, the beginning and the end of everything.[12] Do not harden your hearts and ignore the evidence before your eyes but come to Me, for I am not far away. I am not far off where you cannot reach Me.[13] I am very close to you, only a step away. Take that step of faith and call on Me,[14] and then you will know for sure that I AM, as My Spirit comes to dwell in your heart.[15]

AUTHOR *Lord, why do You say that they have all done wickedly and there is none who does good?*

FATHER My people, your idea of what is good is not My idea of what is good. Your idea of righteousness is not My idea of righteousness. My thoughts are not your thoughts and My ways are not your ways. My ways and My thoughts are much higher than yours.[16] You compare yourselves with each other and say that this one is more righteous than that one, that this one is more holy than that one. You compare like with like, for you are all wicked and evil compared with Me. Why do you compare yourselves with each other when you should compare yourselves to Me? I am the standard,[17] not you. Not one of you comes any where near My standard. I am perfectly holy, perfectly righteous, perfect in every way. Which one of you can match that? No indeed, you cannot. Indeed you are so far from Me that you have lost all sense of what is right and what is wrong. This is why I had to give you My law, to give you a standard to compare yourselves to.[18] Jesus is the only one who fulfilled the requirements of the law,[19] so compare yourselves to Him and not to each other. By My standard you are all corrupt, you have all done abominable works, and there is none who does good. But do not despair, for this is where I come in. This is why you need Me, for I have chosen to give you My righteousness and My holiness[20] so that you can be with Me. This is why I sent My Son Jesus to pay for your wickedness, and to give all who would come to Him the righteousness of God Himself.[21]

Psalm 14:2–3

AUTHOR *Lord, surely there are some people who seek You? What about Your church?*

FATHER My church are now children of God and not children of men.[22] Yes, you are of human birth in your bodies but in your spirit you are a new creation. The old has died and the new has been born.[23] My church are My children born of My Spirit, My sons and daughters, and My heirs.[24] They are not citizens of this world but citizens of My kingdom.[25] My church are aliens in a strange land and they are My ambassadors to the children of men.[26] So, at the time that this scripture was written there was no church and no one had been born anew by My Spirit. Therefore all men were wicked. But now there is a new race,[27] a race of special beings, new creations who are born anew in My likeness. These men are good, these men are righteous and these men do seek after God with all their heart for I have made them so. This scripture therefore is talking only about those sons of men who have not been born anew. Amongst them there is not one who does good, not one who is righteous and not one who seeks after Me. Have I not just said that all men in their natural state are corrupt, totally wicked and depraved, and seek only after their own pleasures, or the will of My enemy Satan.[28] Not one of these children of men seeks after Me, no not one, unless, and I say again, unless I first seek after them. And that I am doing. My eyes run to and fro throughout the whole world, without ceasing, to see if there is anyone to whom I can show mercy.[29] My desire is not to destroy men but to save them, and I will search high and low, in season and out of season, to try and find anyone who will listen to Me when I call them.[30] And I call and call. I call everyone, but not everyone is listening to Me. Only a few are alert enough to hear My voice and when they respond, however minute that response might be, I send My Spirit to that one to draw them closer and closer to Me.[31] As they respond I place in them the desire to seek Me and when they follow that desire I make sure that they find Me.[32] I will not allow anyone to slip through My fingers who will in any way respond to Me. I will draw to Myself all men who will listen to and hear My voice.[33] When finally they make a decision to make Jesus their Lord[34] then I can begin the process of sanctification, making them holy and fit for heaven.[35] But in the natural, left to their own devices there is indeed no one who would seek after Me. There is no one who is righteous or does good. No not one, and unless they will respond to Me and turn from their wicked ways they will indeed suffer the fate that I have ordained for My enemy Satan and his angels.[36] So, you children of men, listen for My voice for I am calling you. Listen to Me and respond to Me and turn from your wicked ways. Seek after Me and you shall find Me, and then I can rescue you and cause you, too, to be born anew and become a citizen of My kingdom and an alien in this wicked world.

Psalm 14:4

AUTHOR *Lord, why do workers of iniquity eat up Your people? What does that mean?*

FATHER As I have said, workers of iniquity have no consciousness of God and therefore they look only to themselves to provide for their needs. It is My desire to meet the needs of people and I have done that from the very beginning. I am Jehovah Jireh, the one who provides.[37] I provided for Adam in the beginning. I gave him all that was necessary to sustain life in glorious abundance and luxury. All he had to do was tend the garden in accordance with My word.[38] He had great knowledge[39] but believed the lie that I was withholding from him.[40] I have never withheld anything good from My people.[41] Adam traded My knowledge for the knowledge of good and evil and as a result he began to lose his God consciousness. Now evildoers have no knowledge of Me at all[42] so how can they believe that I am their provider? Instead they look to themselves and to those around them to provide for their needs and their wants. And because they have no knowledge of Me they seek to take from My people whatever their heart desires. My people are blessed because they trust Me,[43] but evildoers seek to take for themselves what My people have in order to satisfy their own desires, instead of looking to Me to provide for them. They will not cry to Me, they will not call on Me, because they have no knowledge of Me. If they would turn to Me and put their trust in Me and obey My word then I would be their provider too. And then there would be more than enough for everyone, for I create abundance and not lack.[44] There are no shortages in Me or in what I create, but only in what the devil and evildoers have corrupted.[45] Look to Me My people and I will supply all that you need and all that you desire.[46]

Psalm 14:5

AUTHOR *Why are evildoers in great fear?*

FATHER They are in great fear because they have only themselves and their own resources to rely on. When they come to the end of those resources, when the world system's supply runs out, what else is there for them? Where do they turn? What do they do? They seek to gather and gather, hoard and hoard, for great fear is upon them that they may not have enough. They build bigger and bigger barns until they feel secure.[47] They trample on the poor and take from them in order to create abundance for themselves.[48] This is because there is no peace in building bigger barns, there is no peace in hoarding, for what you have gathered and hoarded can so easily be stolen from you.[49] Yes they are in great fear and many cannot withstand the pressure when it seems that the security of this world's system is about to fall. This is so foolish. Why do you put your trust in riches instead of in Me? My supply will not run dry; My economic system will not collapse. Obey My word, do it My way instead of doing it your way, and instead of great fear you shall have great peace as you put your trust in Me.

Psalm 14:6

AUTHOR *Lord, how does the evil man shame the counsel of the poor?*

FATHER The evil man seeks wealth for the wrong reasons. I am not against a man having wealth provided he uses it rightly and justly. Am I not the one who gives you the power to get wealth?[50] Am I not the one who made My friend Abraham exceedingly rich?[51] You too are My friends. Indeed you are My children and My heirs, and therefore I have no problem with you being wealthy for I have created abundance for you. It is the love of money that leads to all kinds of evil,[52] not the money itself. It is a question of your motivation for having wealth and a question of how submitted you are to the leading of My Spirit. Wealth is not a problem in itself. It is a tool to be used wisely for My kingdom. No, the problem is when a man loves money because of the power and the status it will bring him. A rich man who is not being led by My Spirit and who has made his money his god[53] will use that wealth to suppress and oppress the poor. Money gives you the ability to do what you want to do, for that is how the world system works. Now, you can use that wealth to bless others less fortunate than yourself or you can use that wealth to bless yourself. If you will use the wealth that you have to be a blessing to others then I will see to it that you too are blessed.[54] The reason that I made Abraham exceedingly rich was because he would be a blessing to the whole world.[55] I have said that the church will have the blessing of Abraham[56] and that is for the same reason. I expect you to look for opportunities to bless others, those poorer than yourselves.[57] This is what My kingdom and My righteousness is about.[58] Seek first My kingdom and My righteousness, and all these other things I will add to you.[59] But the wicked man, the evildoer, will use his wealth to do the opposite. He will bless himself and oppress others. He will frustrate the plans of the poor because he will use his wealth to strengthen his own power and position at their expense. But let that man beware, for I am the refuge of the poor and of the humble. I will fight on behalf of the righteous man and I will destroy the wealth of the wicked.[60] Indeed I will take his wealth from him and give it to the man who will do justly in My eyes[61] for I am the strong defender of the poor and the oppressed, of the widow and the fatherless.[62]

Psalm 14:7

AUTHOR *Lord, why do You cry for the salvation of Israel to come out of Zion?*

FATHER The Salvation of Israel has already come out of Zion.[63] This word is already fulfilled. My Son Jesus is the salvation of Israel just as He is the salvation of the whole world. But My people Israel do not recognise Him or acknowledge Him. However I am not distressed by this for there is an appointed time and a set time for My chosen people to accept their Messiah.[64] Did not Jesus say that they would not see Him again until they cried, 'Blessed is He who comes in the name of the Lord'.[65] And they will cry this when they look on Him whom they have pierced and their eyes are opened to see who He really is.[66] But My Salvation has come out of Zion and many of you have recognised Him and turned to Him. Blessed are you who have made Him your Lord, and blessed will be My people Israel when they call on Him when He returns to Zion again.

AUTHOR *Lord, what do You mean by saying that Jacob should rejoice and Israel be glad when You bring back the captivity of Your people?*

FATHER My people Israel have been captive amongst the nations for two thousand years and now I am bringing them back to their own land, just as I said that I would.[67] I have not abandoned My people nor forsaken them, because I said that My covenant with them was an everlasting covenant.[68] No I have not abandoned My people. I will still fulfil all My promises to them and they shall still fulfil their destiny to be a blessing to the whole world. Rejoice My people Israel for your captivity is ended. I am bringing you back to your land that I have given to you. Your time of exile is ended and your time of restoration has come. Never again will you be vomited out of your land[69] for I have given it to you as your permanent possession.[70] Rejoice My people Israel for your King is indeed coming to you. Not on a donkey will He come to you this time,[71] but riding on a white horse[72] and you shall indeed look on Him and say, 'Blessed is He who comes in the name of the Lord'. Rejoice O Israel for your time of trouble is almost over and your time of blessing is at hand.

Psalm Fifteen

Psalm 15:1

AUTHOR *Lord, what does it mean to abide in Your tabernacle and dwell in Your holy hill?*

FATHER To abide in My tabernacle is to dwell in My presence. My tabernacle is the place where I meet with the children of men.[1] To abide in My tabernacle is to stay continually in My presence. Many of you spend time in My presence but not many of you abide in My presence. There is a difference. Under the old covenant the high priest came into My presence to perform specific acts as laid down in My law. He performed those acts and then he left the tent of My presence until the next occasion. Many of you do that. You come into My presence for a purpose and then you leave again. This is not what I want, for it means that I only see you on occasions. What I want is to fellowship with you all of the time. Only Moses and Joshua abided in My presence. When Moses came up the mountain he came to abide in My presence for forty days and afterwards his face shone with My glory.[2] Joshua abided in My presence for a time and would not leave the tabernacle.[3] My people, I have given you a new covenant and a better covenant than that. I have made provision for you to be able to stay in My presence all the time.[4] You need never leave My presence, for now I dwell within you and you have become My tabernacle. Your bodies are now the temple of the Holy Spirit and the place where I meet with you.[5] And yet you still only visit Me on occasions. You still only acknowledge Me when you have a duty to perform or when you want something from Me. This is not what I want. This is not why My Son died, why the veil in the temple was destroyed.[6] I have removed the veil that stops you coming into My presence. My Son has opened up a new and living way for you to dwell in My holy hill.[7] You can come right into the throne room, right into the holy of holies, right into My presence, for you are My children[8] and I love to have you with Me. You need never leave My presence for I am in you by My Spirit.[9] And yet you are always leaving Me and going off to do your own thing. You never give Me a thought until you get into trouble or need something from Me, and then you come running back to Me. I am glad that you do that, that you do come back to Me, but how much better it would be if you never left My presence. You do not have to leave My presence when you go about your daily business for I am in you and I go with you. I want you to abide in My presence. I want you to live in My presence. I want you to stay in My presence all the time. This is what the new covenant is about. This is why it is a better covenant with better promises for we can be together all the time.[10] You need never leave

My presence and I can be with you and share in all that you do, for the Holy Spirit lives in you. And through Him My presence goes with you wherever you go.[11] So please do not ignore Me. Instead, will you fellowship with Me all your day? Just talk to Me and listen to Me as you go about your daily business. If you will do this then you too will shine with the light of My presence and the world will know that you and I are one.[12]

Psalm 15:2

AUTHOR *Lord, what does it mean to walk uprightly?*

FATHER He who abides in My presence must walk uprightly, and to walk uprightly means to conduct oneself in a right and proper manner. Your walk is the way in which you pass through this life. It is the way that you conduct yourself in your relationship with Me and with others. To walk is to progress and to pass along and pass through this life. There is a right and a wrong way to do this. To be upright means to conduct yourself in accordance with My word. I have laid down in My word the standards that I expect you to keep, both in your relationship to Me and to each other. See that you study My word and renew your mind so that you know what I require of you.[13] This is your responsibility, your part to play. If you will do this then I will see to it that you have the power and the ability to walk the walk that I have called you to walk.[14] If you are to abide in My presence and if I am to be with you at all times, then you must walk as I would walk. Let your conduct be as Mine would be.

This is not an impossible task for you because I am in you and with you, to give you the power and ability to do this. This is why I give grace to you. My grace is sufficient for you in your weakness.[15] It is in My strength and My ability that you will do this and not your own. All I require from you is that you have a willing heart and that you renew your mind with My word so that you will know what I require of you. My Spirit is in you and My grace will do the rest.

AUTHOR *Lord, what does it mean to work righteousness?*

FATHER I want you to have a pure heart. Your motives will determine the way in which you conduct your walk. Out of a right spirit will come a righteous walk and out of a wrong spirit will come an evil walk. So allow Me to check your motives and correct you if necessary. Keep checking with Me and I will show you if you have gone astray. Listen for the voice behind you saying, 'This is the way, walk in it', and then repent.[16] Turn back onto the right path and your walk will be righteous. As your motives are righteous so your deeds, or your works, will be righteous too; for a heart that is righteous will produce works that are righteous. Again, let Me do this in you. It is not by might, nor by power, but by My Spirit.[17] It is not in your own strength that you will accomplish this but by My Spirit working in you to perfect that righteousness in you.[18]

AUTHOR *Lord, and what about speaking the truth in our hearts?*

FATHER What is truth? I am the truth.[19] My words are the truth. Speak according to My word. You must know My word to know what is true. Many things that the world declare as truth are not in fact truth when checked against My word. The world's truth is perverted and far from My truth. Again, motivation is so important. What are your true motives? You can do right things with wrong motives and make truth a lie. The world's truth is a deception. Do not be fooled by what the world declares to be true. You must re-program your mind with My word and then you will know what is good and perfect and acceptable to Me.[20] Let what resides in your heart and what comes out of your mouth be My truth, for by your words you will be justified and by your words you will be condemned.[21] The words that you speak will be an indication of what is in your heart, for out of the abundance of the heart the mouth speaks.[22] Let My truth dwell richly in you.[23] Let My truth be in your mind and in your heart at all times. Do not be conformed to this world but renew your mind with My word and be transformed. Let the words that you speak be My words,[24] let the deeds that you do be My deeds,[25] let the way that you walk be My way,[26] and you shall abide in My tabernacle at all times.

Psalm 15:3

AUTHOR *Lord, what does it mean to backbite with our tongue?*

FATHER My children, your tongues are the most dangerous weapon that you have. The tongue is one of the smallest parts of the body, but it can do untold damage if not used rightly.[27] Think about it. I have told you that what you believe in your heart and say with your mouth you shall have.[28] Do you really want what you say to come to pass? If you could have everything that you say come to pass immediately what sort of state would you be in? What sort of state would others be in as a result of what you have just said, if it came to pass immediately? Do you remember the story called 'The Midas Touch', where the king thought that it would be wonderful if everything he touched turned to gold?[29] What riches he would have. But what was the reality? A nightmare beyond anything he imagined, for everything he touched instantly became gold, including his food and including his children. What would be the result if everything that you said immediately came to pass? Remember that life and death are in the power of the tongue.[30] What you say may not happen immediately but happen it will if you keep on saying it long enough.

O My people watch the words that come out of your mouth. Just take notice for a while and see if indeed you really want what you say to happen. You are so careless about what you say. You are so destructive in what you say, both about yourselves and about others. What will the words that you have just spoken bring? Will they bring blessing or bring cursing?[31] Will they build up or will they tear down? How do you speak about your brothers and sisters to other people? How do you speak about the world to others? How do you speak about the people that I have put in authority over your nation? Your words do create and bring about the things that you say, for I have made you in My image[32] and I create things by the words that I speak. Did I not say, 'Light be', and there was light?[33] You too, because you are created like Me, have the power to create through the words that you speak. The results may not be instantaneous in your case but you will reap what you say. Your tongue has the power to create, either for good or for evil. You can steer the course of your life, or the lives or others, by the words that you speak.[34] I cannot emphasise this enough, My people. Be careful what you speak, for your words will create what you say, for good or for evil. This is why I want you to speak My words. This is why I want you to renew your minds and fill your hearts with My words, so that when you open your mouths to speak, what will come out will be wholesome, uplifting and edifying.[35] Every time you speak I want what you say to be in line with My word and then you will not add to the evil and the confusion that is already in the world. Speak good things, My people. Speak good things only. Build up and do not pull down. If you can't say something good then don't say anything at all.

Listen to what I am saying. You cannot spend time in My presence, you cannot abide in My tabernacle, if the words that come from your mouth are only evil continually. And by evil words I mean words that are contrary to what I have already written. And by contrary I mean words that are both the opposite of what I have said and words that are spoken in an opposite spirit to that in which I said them. The way that you speak them, as well as the words themselves, must be in line with My word and the character of My Spirit. Be warned, you will be judged for every idle word that you speak.[36] By idle words I mean words that do not create, that are non productive, or those that produce wrong results. These are evil words. Even though they may be true in the natural, they may not agree with what I have written. For example, the ten spies who went into the Promised Land came back with a report that was true in the natural, but it was nevertheless an evil report for they said, 'We are not able', and I had said that I had already given them the land. Only Joshua and Caleb reported the truth for they said, 'We are well able'.[37] So I consider any word that you speak that is contrary to what I have already said in My word to be an evil word. So My people be very careful what you say, both about yourselves and about each other. There is nothing that distresses Me more than hearing the evil words that so many of you speak so much of the time, for you are creating what you say and you will ultimately have what you say unless you repent and change the confession that comes out of your mouth. Let your tongue be a creative force for good and not for evil.

AUTHOR *And what about doing evil to our neighbours?*

FATHER I have already told you in the story of the Good Samaritan how I expect you to treat your neighbour.[38] There are only two commandments on which all the law and the prophets hang. The first is to love Me with all your mind, all your soul and all of your being. If you will love Me with everything that is in you then you will automatically fulfil the second, and that is to love your neighbour as yourself.[39] If you will do this then you will abide in My presence, for I am love. You cannot love Me unless that love is expressed to those around you. If you love Me you will abide in My presence, and if you abide in My presence you will love those around you, for I am love.[40]

AUTHOR *Lord, what does it mean to take up a reproach against a friend?*

FATHER Do not receive it. If someone speaks evil of a brother or a neighbour refuse to listen. Refuse to accept what they say. I hate tale telling.[41] Especially do I hate tale telling when it is in the guise of telling someone some tasty trifle about a brother or sister, 'so that they can pray about it'. Check your motives. Why do you need to say anything at all if it does not build up, and why do you need to listen if someone seeks to speak evil to you of another?[42] My people, you must stop the gossip. It is so destructive. It goes the rounds like wild fire. That tongue of yours can start a huge blaze from just one tiny spark of gossip and indiscretion.[43] I hate it, for people and ministries are destroyed as a result of idle words. Do not let the enemy bring destruction. Determine in your hearts that you will neither speak anything, nor listen to anything that is spoken, against another. Do not receive it and do not speak it. If no one speaks and no one listens then the fire can be extinguished before it even starts. I am serious about this, My people. I hate gossip. I hate evil speaking, and I will not tolerate it in My presence. I will not fellowship with anyone who sows discord amongst the brethren or who uses his tongue to bring destruction to another.[44] I have given you your tongue and your ability to speak so that you can bring life and blessing to those around you, not cursing and death. Learn to speak right things, My people, if you want to abide in My presence.

Psalm 15:4

AUTHOR *Lord, what does it mean to despise a vile person?*

JESUS My people, I have separated you and set you apart as a people who are dedicated to Me. I have made you a royal priesthood and My own special people.[45] You are sanctified and set apart for Me. Therefore I expect you to reject that which belongs to the world or is associated with the world.[46] You cannot conform to the world and be set apart for Me.[47] It has to be either one or the other. I have called you out of the world and therefore you must separate yourself from the things that those in the world do. You cannot have a foot in both camps. You cannot serve the world and serve Me.[48] Make up your minds who is your Lord and in which kingdom you belong. If you belong to Me then you must reject the world and its way of doing things, for the world and its system of doing things, its values, its morals and its standards are not of Me. Turn your back on the world and set your face steadfastly towards My kingdom. Do not associate yourselves with the world. Hate the vile person who follows the world's standards and love Me. Reject the vile person and love Me. Despise the things that the vile person does. Despise the things that he believes in. Despise his values; despise what he sets his eyes on. Despise what he opens his ears to. Despise the places he frequents and separate yourselves from him and be holy unto Me. Follow My ways, My teachings and My standards. Be holy, for I am holy[49] and you belong to Me, for I have bought you with a price.[50] I have redeemed you and set you free from slavery to the world's system.[51] So why do you still behave as the vile man does? Why do you still associate with him, frequent his places of entertainment, watch what he watches and listen to what he listens to? No, My people, I am perfecting holiness in you. The world must look on you and see that you are different. They must see that you are holy and set apart for Me. Yes they will criticise you, yes they will mock you, yes they will say that you are fanatical, that you have gone too far and that you have become religious nuts, but let them. What is more important to you, the approval of a vile man or the approval of the Lord your God? Of course vile men will mock you, for you challenge them and make them uncomfortable. That is why they persecuted Me. But I have called you out to be My bride and I expect you to forsake your father's house and join yourself to Me.[52] Love Me. Do not love the world. Do not love the vile person who seeks only to do his own will and the will of Satan his father.[53] Hate the vile person. Do not love him. Now, do not misunderstand Me. I am not telling you to hate a man. I love all men and desire all men to be saved.[54] I am telling you to hate what the vile man stands for, what motivates him and what he takes pleasure in. When I say to hate the vile man I mean that you should not join him in his evil ways. I want you to be separate from him and firmly established in My kingdom and in My righteousness so that you can pray for the vile man, and so that you can tell him of the things of God without you becoming contaminated by him. I need you to be able to go into the places of darkness without becoming part of them. I need you to be able to take a light in there so that the darkness will be dispelled and the vile man will be able to see clearly and turn from his wicked ways.[55] For you to do this you must be light. You must be totally separate from him so that your light is distinguishable from his darkness. Therefore, My people, hate the vile man, despise him and keep yourselves separate and holy, set apart for Me to be a light in the darkness. If you will do this you will abide in My tabernacle and dwell in My holy hill.

AUTHOR *What about honouring those who fear the Lord?*

JESUS Who are your role models, My people? Who do you look up to? Who do you copy? Who do you desire to be like? Paul said to the church at Corinth that they should imitate him, as he imitated Me.[56] I want you to do likewise. Look at those who are walking closely with Me. Look at their lifestyle and seek to do likewise. Let them be an example to you and honour them. Set your focus on Me, as seen in them, and seek to live godly and holy lives as befits a people called to be My bride.

AUTHOR *What do You mean for us to swear to our own hurt and not change?*

FATHER I mean for you to honour your word. Let your 'yes' be yes and your 'no' be no.[57] Be like Me. I am not a man that I should lie. What I have said, that I will do.[58] I will not change that which has come out of My mouth.[59] Because My word is My bond you can fully trust and rely on what I have written. I will not go back on anything that I have said in My word even though it might cost Me dearly. Indeed I have already proved this, for I said, before I even created you, that

I would rescue you from the clutches of the enemy and that I would make you My children, and that I would do it through the death and resurrection of My Son.[60] And it cost Me dearly to keep My word, but I did keep it. That is one of the reasons why Jesus had to drink the cup that I had given Him for there was no other way, for I had spoken.[61] So, My people, I want you to consider carefully before you open your mouths, and when you have spoken I want you to honour what you say. Be without shadow of turning as I do not turn.[62] As I do not deviate from My word then I want you to do the same. Let men know that you mean what you say and that you are reliable, even if it should cost you to do so. You are My representatives, so be like Me and represent Me to the world faithfully.

Psalm 15:5

AUTHOR *Lord, how does not putting out our money at usury relate to us?*

JESUS My children, freely you have received, freely give.[63] I am not concerned about you trying to make money out of the world system for the wealth of the sinner is laid up for the just,[64] and it is My intention that the wealth of the world should come into My church,[65] so that My church will have the necessary funds to preach the gospel throughout the earth before I come. I understand that you need money to do this. Neither am I concerned that you receive reward for work that you do, for the labourer is worthy of his hire.[66] What does concern Me is that you should seek to make money out of your brothers and sisters at their expense and for your benefit.[67] You are where you are now in My kingdom because I freely gave to you. I did not charge you for your salvation but I gave it to you as a free gift. In return I want you to freely give to others so that they too can have the opportunity to hear the gospel. It is a question of motivation again, as it usually is. To put out your money to usury means that your motivation is to bless yourself rather than the other person. It is self-centred and that is not My way. That is the way of the world. We are not just talking about money here but we are talking about general principles. What is your motivation? Where is your heart? If your heart is one with Mine then your motivation will be to give, your motivation will be to bless, and not to seek reward for yourself. My kingdom principles are the opposite of those in the world. The people of the world are self-centred and they always seek to bless themselves first. They think only of what they can get and not of what they can give. And as you know, it is the love of money, and more than the money itself it is the power and authority it brings with it, that is the root of all kinds of evil.[68] My children you are in My kingdom now and I expect you to live by My principles. I expect you to have My heart, and that is a heart to give and to bless. If you will seek My kingdom first I will ensure that all the other things that you need will come to you.[69] You see, I have built into My kingdom the principle of sowing and reaping.[70] Whatever you sow, that shall you reap.[71] Therefore if you give, it will be given to you; good measure, pressed down, shaken together and running over shall be given to you.[72] If you will seek to bless others then I will cause others to bless you, and just as the five loaves and two fish were multiplied when they were given so I will cause what you give to multiply and multiply.[73] At usury you will only get a percentage interest on what you loan. If you will give freely I can multiply and multiply. If My church will get hold of this principle then I can keep multiplying what they keep giving and I can cause wealth and riches to come to you, for I know that I can trust you to keep giving and giving. My people, keep giving freely and lending freely, not just of your money but of anything and everything that I have entrusted you with. Have My heart. As you have freely received then freely give. Look for ways to bless others and I will find ways to bless you.

AUTHOR *Lord, You said that you were not concerned about us trying to make money out of the world system. This sounds a bit like You are telling us to exploit people in the world instead of blessing them. Can You clarify this.*

JESUS No, I am not telling you to exploit people. That is totally contrary to My nature. What I am saying is this: that the world has developed a system of finance for itself and this system is contrary to the kingdom of heaven in that it works from a different motivation, a motivation of blessing self. However I have no objection to you using the system that the world has developed, providing that you do so legitimately and in line with My principles.[74] Did I not give to you the parable of the talents? I commended those who put out the money I had given them to gain interest and I condemned the man who did nothing.[75] Use the world's system but use it in conjunction with kingdom principles. I am the one who gives you the power to get wealth so that I can establish My covenant in the earth.[76] As I have said, I intend that the wealth of the sinner will come to those who will use it righteously for My kingdom. Wealth is a tool to be used and I have no problem with that. It is you who have a problem with money. Money in itself is neither good nor evil. It is the motivation in your heart that is a matter of good and evil. So, no, I don't want you to exploit people in the world, but there is no reason why you cannot use the world's system to bring money to yourselves and into the kingdom, for I know that as My people you are submitted to My Lordship and you will handle that wealth as I direct you. I will only give you what you can handle without you becoming corrupted. This is why I gave five talents to one man, two to another and to the third man, just one. I know you, My people. I know what you can deal with and I know where your heart is. I will deal with each one of you in accordance with the condition of your heart. So do not be afraid of money. Do not be afraid of wealth, for it is but a tool for you to use rightly in the furtherance of My kingdom on this earth.

AUTHOR *Lord, what does it mean to take a bribe against the innocent?*

JESUS My people, why are you so ready to speak evil of one another?[77] Why are you so eager to sow discord among the brethren?[78] Why are you so keen to pull each other down instead of building each other up?[79] Why will you listen with burning ears to every tale that is told against a brother?[80] Why do you allow Satan to bribe you with cheap glory as you pass on that tasty titbit of gossip?[81] Do not testify against each other. Do not tell to others what you know of a brother that will be to his detriment. Build up and do not tear down. Let your testimony be of good things that will lift a brother up in the eyes of his brethren. O My children, I hate it when you seek to destroy each other, when with glee you spread evil gossip against each other. Do not be bribed; do not be persuaded to speak that which is against another. If you have a genuine complaint then I have laid down procedures in My word whereby you should seek recourse.[82] If someone has wronged you then do what I have told you to do.[83] If a brother falls into sin then come to Me about it and pray to Me for that brother.[84] Intercede for him and do not spread evil reports about him. Remember that a report can be evil even when it is true, if it is given from a wrong motive. Remember, My children, that but for the grace of God in your lives you would all go the same way. It is only by grace that you have been saved[85] and it is only by grace that you can work out your salvation.[86] Do not judge each other therefore, for as you judge others so will you yourselves be judged.[87] You have only one judge and that is Me,[88] so come to Me with your problems, with your complaints and with your troubles. Come to Me and pour out your hearts to Me and not to each other for I can keep a secret.[89] I can keep close counsel and I will redeem the matter[90] instead of spreading evil reports that will bring discord among the brethren. O My children, this matter is so close to My heart, that of how you speak to each other and about each other. In the times that are coming on the earth you will have tribulation enough from the enemy[91] without you seeking to destroy each other. Please will you listen to what I say and repent of your evil words. Purify your mouths and speak with clean lips[92] for you need to edify each other and to build each other up, for you are all My body on this earth and I have prayed that you will be one.[93] Seek unity, My brethren, for where there is unity there the anointing oil will flow and there I will command the blessing.[94] If you are to stand against the enemy then you must stand together in unity[95] supporting and encouraging each other and lifting each other up when you fall,[96] for fall indeed you will from time to time.[97] I do not condemn you so neither shall you condemn each other.[98] Determine now that from this day forward you will be a people of pure hearts and clean lips and I will abide with you, and you shall dwell in My holy hill, and I will command the blessing upon you so that you can faithfully represent Me to the world. He who does these things that I have talked to you about will abide in My tabernacle forever, but if you ignore what I say and do those things that I detest then I will surely cast you from My presence, for you who do these things will have no part in Me.[99] If you will obey My word then I will see to it that you will stand firm and stand strong, and that the enemy will have no hold over you. Indeed, the one who does these things that I have commanded shall never be moved and you will be one with Me forever.

Psalm Nineteen

Psalm 19:1

AUTHOR *Lord, how do the heavens declare Your glory and the firmament show Your handiwork?*

FATHER As I have said to you before, the whole of creation speaks of Me.[1] I have a voice in this world that declares to the peoples of this earth that I am God and that I do exist. Just look at the sun, just look at the sky and wonder at it. Does it not speak to you of Me? Of course it does, if you would but open your eyes and see, if you would but set aside your own puny intellects and stop trying to reason away everything that your spirit accepts. Why will you not believe what your eyes see and what your spirit sees? But I have placed a voice in the heavens that speaks of Me and you will hear it if you open your ears to hear what I am saying through My creation.

Psalm 19:2

FATHER Look at the night sky, look at the day, how they follow on from one another in perfect order and in perfect harmony. Look at the stars, look at the moon. See how they are all positioned; just the right size, and just the right distance from the earth to provide you with heat and light; not too much, not too little. See how the clouds form and bring rain. Look at how just the right balance of gasses are in the atmosphere. Study it and wonder. All these things, and much more, are a voice that speaks of Me, that cries out that I am, and if only you would listen you would hear it and know that I am God[2] and that I love you and that you are Mine.

Psalm 19:3–4

FATHER There is nowhere that you can go where the day and the night do not speak to you of Me.[3] The whole of My creation is a voice that declares to you that I am. And I will hold you to account if you ignore what My creation says to you, for I have given you that voice so that you may know Me and turn to Me and be saved from the fate that I have decreed for My enemy Satan and those who follow him and who choose to stand against Me. So listen, open your ears, open your eyes and hear and see what I am saying to you through the voice of the day and the voice of the night, for their cry rings out in silence across this earth declaring to you that I AM indeed.

Psalm 19:4–5

AUTHOR *Lord, what do You mean by saying that the sun is like a bridegroom coming out of his chamber?*

FATHER I have set the sun in the sky to give you light, to give you heat and to give you life,[4] for without the sun there would be no life. The sun, My people, is a picture of My Son Jesus who is your Lord and Saviour. Without Him there is no light in this world. Without Him there is only darkness and no one can see, for He is the light of the world.[5] When He appears there will be no need for the sun, for His glory will be your light.[6] But for now He brings spiritual light into spiritual darkness[7] and gives you revelation and understanding, but when He comes He will shine brighter than a thousand suns[8] and the sun and the moon will no longer show their light.[9] My Son is also your life. Without Him there is no life but only death. He is the resurrection and He is the life[10] and without Him nothing can exist or live.[11] He is your life and He is your light and the sun is a prophetic picture of Him. He is the Day Star[12] and He is rising in the east to declare that the dawn is coming. And then the Sun of Righteousness will arise with healing in His wings,[13] to bring life and health to all those who will turn to Him. Like a bridegroom coming for his bride will the Sun of Righteousness climb across the heavens. As the dawn appears and Jesus comes in great glory to this earth so will the Bridegroom come for His Bride. Like a strong man He will rejoice as He defeats His enemies with the word that comes forth from His mouth.[14] Yes, the Sun of Righteousness has a voice and as He appears He will declare righteousness to be the standard. He will declare righteousness to be the plummet and justice to be the measuring line,[15] and all of you will be judged by that standard. Blessed are you who have made Him to be your righteousness,[16] for healing will be in His wings for you.

Psalm 19:6

FATHER His rising will be from one end of heaven to the other.[17] As the sun rises in the east and sets in the west encircling the whole globe, so will the coming of the Sun of Righteousness be. His glory will encompass the whole earth and all will see Him as the darkness is dispelled for ever.[18] Nothing will remain hidden when He comes,[19] for all will be exposed in the brilliant light of His presence as He tracks His way across the sky from east to west – only My Sun will not set. The darkness will not return, and only the sons of the light will not be burned by the heat of His rising.[20] As He appears He will be as a burning oven to those who are of the darkness.[21] They will be consumed by His coming, all those who love darkness rather than light. Be children of the day, My people.[22] Be not children of the night, for the night is fleeing away as My Son comes in all His glory. Be children of the day, be children of the light, and come to Him now, and let Him purify you now,[23] so that you will not be consumed when the Sun of Righteousness rises as a burning oven over this earth, establishing righteousness in the earth for ever more.[24] Yes, the sun is rising. See, the day star is visible, declaring that the sun has begun its journey across the heavens. Though it still be night now on the earth, soon, very soon, the night will flee away and the day of righteousness will dawn on the earth.

Psalm 19:7

AUTHOR *Father, what do You mean by Your law being perfect and converting the soul?*

FATHER My law, or My word, is perfect. It is complete, it is entire, and it is the truth.[25] It has been refined in the fire and purified seven times.[26] It is therefore completely pure and without error. If people will turn to My word and accept it for what it is, My word to them, they will be comforted, they will be restored and they will be perfected by it. I have given you My word so that you can partake of My wisdom and My knowledge, and so that you can know Me. If you will hear My word and do My word, you will find that your soul, that is, your mind, will and emotions, will be restored and converted so that you begin to think like Me and act like Me. My word is sure; it will not fail, for I have spoken it and I do not lie.[27] My word is a lamp to your feet to give you light and understanding so that you can walk in right paths,[28] be wise and have good success in all that you do.[29]

Psalm 19:8

FATHER The statutes that I have given you are righteous and they will rejoice your heart if you will do them. Many of you think that I have given you rules and regulations to stop you enjoying yourselves, to restrict you and to make your life a misery. This is so far from the truth. I have no wish to stop you enjoying yourselves. I delight in you and I long for you to be blessed. How many of you parents want to spoil your children's fun? No you do not, yet you give them rules to obey, things to do and things not to do. Why do you do this? It is because you seek to protect them from dangers that they are not aware of. You want them to enjoy life without harm and hurt coming to them. So you give them statutes to obey for their protection, to enable them to enjoy life to the full, for you are much wiser than they, you have more knowledge than they, and you are well aware of the pitfalls of life that they have no knowledge of. You love them and therefore you protect them and give them guidelines that will ensure that they are kept safe and are able to reach their full potential. You put restrictions on their behaviour because you love them. Do I not love you, My children? Am I not wiser than you, My children?[30] Is My knowledge not greater than yours, and therefore I seek to protect you? I have given you statutes and I have given you boundaries because I love you and I want you to be protected from the enemy who seeks to destroy you.[31] It is not because I want to restrict you and spoil your fun that I have done this but because I want you to enjoy life and have it in all its fullness.[32] It is because I want you to reach your full potential that I have put in place statutes and commandments. Do not rebel against the pricks, My children.[33] They are there for your benefit, and if you will obey My word your heart will rejoice indeed because you shall have such blessing that you will not be able to contain it.[34] My commandments are indeed pure and they will enlighten your eyes. You will be able to see clearly how to walk, and where to walk, if you will obey them. They shall be a light to your path, and you will not stumble in the darkness[35] for I will be able to direct your steps,[36] if you will obey My word that I have given to you because of My great love for you, My children.

Psalm 19:9

AUTHOR *Father, what do You mean by saying that the fear of the Lord is clean?*

FATHER My children; I want you to reverence Me. So many of you treat Me lightly and have no fear of Me.[37] Now I do not want you to be afraid of Me, for I am your loving heavenly Father, but you do need to understand who I am. I am your Father, yes, but I am also the Lord God Almighty, the maker of heaven and earth. I am Jehovah, the Self-existent and Eternal One and I am so far above you in everything. You need to understand this. You need to understand My holiness and My awesome power. I created everything by the word that came from My mouth, and I can destroy everything in an instant by a word spoken from My mouth. I am your Father but I am not your sugar-daddy. I am not your Santa Claus in the sky. I was not created so that I could bless you, but I created you to bless Me. And bless Me you do, when you obey My word. But do not think that you can continue to disregard Me and disobey My commands with impunity. I have been very tolerant of you so far, but as My glory rises in the earth in these last days you will not be able to treat My presence lightly or with disrespect. I am speaking to you My church, to those of you who know Me. I am not speaking to the world out there but I am speaking to you My children. Remember Ananias and Sapphira.[38] Those days are returning, says your Lord, when great fear came upon the church. My people it is time for you to cease playing with My word, to cease playing with the anointing. The time for irreverence is over. It is time for you to fear Me again. It is time for you to reverence Me again in awesome wonder. It is time for you to know who I am and to obey My word without question. The time for you to pick and choose what you will obey, or not obey, is at an end. Why is this? It is because I want to pour out My power upon you so that you can bring the nations to Me. How can I pour out My power and My anointing upon you when I cannot trust you to obey Me? I need you to fear Me because I need you to obey Me. And I need you to obey Me so that you will be made clean. How can I fill dirty vessels with My power and anointing, for you will corrupt them? When My presence was with the church in those first days that which was corrupt was destroyed in an instant. Remember again Ananias and Sapphira. I need My church to be pure and holy, for the anointing that I am about to pour out on you will be seven times greater than that of those days.[39] I am about to bring together both the former and the latter rain,[40] and My church must be pure and holy in order to contain it. Therefore fear Me, reverence Me, and obey Me, and you shall be clean forever.

AUTHOR *Lord, what about Your judgements being true and righteous?*

FATHER My standards are pure, they are holy and they are righteous. I judge according to My standard. You may not understand, and you may question, but know that My thoughts are higher than yours and My ways are higher than your ways. Trust Me. I make right judgements and right decisions. Do not go by your own judgements but trust Me. Lean on Me and agree with Me. Agree with My word and do what I say and you will have nothing to fear and you will have good success. Remember that I judge in your favour, for you are Mine and I love you. I am not seeking to condemn but to bless.[41]

Psalm 19:10

AUTHOR *Lord, why are Your judgements to be desired more than gold?*

FATHER Gold is precious; it has worth and value and it gives power to those who possess it. My commandments and My judgements have great value too, for they will give wisdom to those who possess them.[42] They will give power to those who possess them and they will give the ability to prosper to those who do them. My statutes are of much more value than gold for they give you access to My mind and to My kingdom, and I am the originator of all wealth and all success and prosperity.[43] If you will take hold of My word, and do it, then you will find it precious indeed, for in it are the precepts for life.[44] Gold can give you power but it cannot give you wisdom, and power without wisdom can cause a person to self-destruct, for power without wisdom will corrupt even the most righteous of men, whereas wisdom will give you a firm foundation on which to build that power.

Wisdom will enable you to operate in My power, and My power coupled with My wisdom will not corrupt. So seek wisdom and not gold, for wisdom will bring the gold. Solomon asked for wisdom rather than gold, and because he did so I gave him the gold also.[45] As long as he continued to obey My word he remained blessed. It was when he turned away from doing My word that he became corrupted.[46] So seek after My word, My precepts and My judgements, and I will give you the gold. My judgements are much more precious to you than fine gold for in them you will find the meaning of life.

AUTHOR *Lord, why are they sweeter than honey?*

FATHER Riches will taste sweet but they will bring bitterness to the soul if there is no wisdom. Wisdom is sweet indeed to the spirit and there is no sorrow with it.[47]

Psalm 19:11

AUTHOR *Lord, what do You mean by Your servant being warned?*

FATHER Your enemy, Satan, roams about like a roaring lion looking for someone to devour.[48] He operates by deceit and lies.[49] He speaks a form of truth but twists it so that the unwary are deceived.[50] My word will warn you when he is trying to deceive you, for you can check what he says against My word. If My word is embedded in your heart you will be able to spot a word of deception immediately. Even if he should appear as an angel of light[51] you will know it is him by the words that he speaks, for his words will not be true to My word. My word will warn you when you are about to step from the right path and the narrow way. You will hear a voice behind you saying, 'This is the way, walk in it'.[52] My word is your guide and your foundation. Do My word and you will not be led astray. Therefore rejoice in My commandments for they are life to you.[53] They will keep you from the snare of the fowler and the clutches of the evil one.[54]

AUTHOR *And what about there being great reward in keeping them?*

FATHER Yes, there is great reward in keeping them. Have I not said that this is so? There is great blessing to be had when you obey My word. You will be blessed going out and coming in. Indeed you will be blessed in every area of your life,[55] if you will study and learn and do My word, for in My word, as I have said, lies the foundation of life.[56]

Psalm 19:12

AUTHOR *Lord, is it right that we cannot understand our errors?*

JESUS A blind man cannot see. I have come to lead you into the light. The heart of man is desperately wicked and who can understand it.[57] Adam believed that eating the fruit of the tree of the knowledge of good and evil would give him understanding and insight into the realm of the spirit. He believed that he would be as God and understand all mysteries.[58] But instead it caused him to become blind and cut off from his Father and the wisdom of the Holy One. Instead of being able to see more clearly Adam became blind and could not see at all. That is the state of people in the world to this day. They think that they are wise and have great insight but in reality they are blind and have no understanding.[59] This is why I have sent the Holy Spirit into the world, to convict people of their sin.[60] One of His jobs is to open the eyes of the spiritually blind so that they can see again. When a man responds to Me then My Spirit will begin to work in that man to open his eyes and show him that he is indeed a sinner. The Holy Spirit will bring revelation to that man of his true condition before Me, so that he can repent and be forgiven. A man cannot repent until he has a revelation of his true state, and the god of this world has blinded the eyes of men so that they should not see, and so that they are deceived into believing that they are righteous in My sight and able to enter heaven.[61] Pray for these people that their eyes will be opened, that they may see and repent and be saved.

AUTHOR *Lord, will You cleanse us from our secret faults?*

JESUS Of course I will. That is My desire for you, that you will be set free and restored to fellowship with Me and your Father. This is why I came; to destroy the works of the evil one.[62] It is not Our desire to punish man for his evil deeds. It is not Our desire to send men to hell.[63] Your Father is not sitting in judgement over you, just waiting for you to slip up so that He has an excuse to destroy you. He has no need of such an excuse or reason, for you yourselves have provided the reason and you have destroyed yourselves. No, Our desire is not to condemn you but to save you. Our purpose is not to judge you, for I have been judged in your place, I have been condemned in your place.[64] Do you not understand the heart of your Father? Your Father is love and He loves you with an everlasting love, a love that drove Him to punish Me in your place so that you could be set free from the consequences of your sin.[65] And My love for you is such that I agreed to suffer in your place. I agreed to take your sin on Me so that you could have My righteousness[66] and sit with Me in heavenly places, with your Father and My Father.[67] Do not ever think that We are seeking to condemn you. All We want is for you to acknowledge that you have sinned and gone your own way, and for you to repent and turn back to Us and We will set you free.[68] We will reinstate you into a relationship with Us. Indeed We will go even better than that; We will make you Our children[69] and My bride.[70] All you have to do is repent and say, 'Father forgive me', and We will make you clean again. Indeed it will be as though you had never sinned. All your sin will be washed away by My blood that was shed in the place of yours.[71] And it doesn't matter what you have done; there is no sin so great that you cannot be cleansed. Never think that you are beyond reach. No one, I say no one, whatever they have done, is beyond the reach of My blood. All can be cleansed and made new again just as though you had never sinned. And neither does it matter how often you sin for you can still be cleansed.[72] Now I am not saying that you can go on sinning deliberately and treat as nothing the sacrifice that I have made on your behalf.[73] No, I'm not saying that. You cannot be led by the Spirit of God and keep on deliberately sinning[74] and think that it will all be all right in the end. No it will not, for if you are not led by the Spirit then you are not a son of your Father, and if you are not His son you will have no part of Him. No, I am talking about you making mistakes and falling, for you will all do that. But if you are being led by the Spirit then He will lead you into repentance.[75] Indeed He will show you the moment you slip up and fail, and He will lead you to repent the moment He reveals to you your error.[76] Sin will greatly distress you if you are a son of your Father and in that case He will forgive you the moment you repent. Keep short accounts. Do not let your sin go on unforgiven, for if you do you will separate yourself from your Father's love and He doesn't want that. So listen to the Spirit. He will show you your hidden faults. When He does, then repent and you will instantly be forgiven and all will be well. Remember at all times that your Father is not out to condemn you[77] but to love you and bring you back into fellowship with Him.

Psalm 19:13

AUTHOR *Lord, what does it mean for You to keep me back from presumptuous sins and for them not to have dominion over me?*

FATHER My son, I cannot keep you from presumptuous sin. This is a matter for you, for a presumptuous sin is one that comes from your own will and out of your own arrogance and pride. A presumptuous sin is one that you will commit when you allow your own thoughts and desires to take precedence over My word. My word is your standard. I have given you My word to keep you in the truth. Submit yourself to My word which is useful for correction and instruction.[78] An arrogant man is one who exalts his own thoughts above My word. A truly humble man is one who will submit his own thoughts and ideas and desires to the authority of My word. I rejoice in a humble man for he will not commit presumptuous sins. Jesus was truly humble for He submitted everything He did and everything He spoke to the authority of My word, even though He was the Word made flesh.[79] Renew your mind[80] and bring every thought captive and submit it to My word[81] and then you will not sin. Sin occurs when you exalt your own thoughts above My word and meditate on them. As you meditate on those thoughts they will create a desire in you which will lead you to sin.[82] So My son, if you want to stay free from presumptuous sin, and all sin is presumptuous sin, for all sin is a result of exalting your own thoughts and ideas above Mine, if you want to stay free then think My thoughts and let My word be what you meditate on, and let My word be your guide and instructor. If you will do this then sin can have no hold on you and it will not have dominion over you. Then you shall be blameless and innocent of great transgression. When you do fail, as you will, then quickly repent, turn back to Me and I will cause you to be clean again.

Psalm 19:14

AUTHOR *Lord, what words of my mouth and meditations of my heart are acceptable in Your sight?*

FATHER The words of your mouth and the meditations of your heart that are acceptable in My sight are those that are in line with My word, which I have already spoken to you and written down for you. Re-program your mind with My word and then you shall know My mind.[83] Speak My word when you open your mouth. You do not necessarily need to quote scripture all the time, but what you say must be in line with My word. You should be able to support everything that you say from the scripture. Let nothing come out of your mouth which does not agree with what I have written. And what comes out of your mouth will be what you have put into your heart.[84] So meditate My word, chew it over, mutter it to yourself. Let it consume you and you consume it. If you will make My word a very part of you then your meditations will be acceptable in My sight and the words of your mouth will delight Me, for what you believe in your heart and confess with your mouth you shall have.[85]

AUTHOR *Lord, what does it mean for You to be My strength and redeemer?*

FATHER I am your strength. I do not expect you to succeed in your own strength. I expect you to be willing to obey Me and I expect you to ask Me to help you. If you will ask, I will help. This is why I have sent My Spirit, the Helper, to be with you.[86] So do not try to rely on your own strength. Submit yourself to My word, be willing to obey Me and ask Me to accomplish it in you. This is what grace is for, to give you the power to fulfil My commands. I know you are incapable of doing so in your own strength. Have you not proved this so often? No, I don't expect you to succeed on your own. I will make you succeed if you will submit to Me and be humble.[87] The proud and the arrogant will try to please Me in their own strength but they will fall, for I will let them fall until they turn to Me and ask for My help. And when they do I shall redeem them. I will pick them up and place their feet back on the rock of My word where their lives will be built upon a solid foundation.[88] Yes, I am your strength and I am your redeemer. I am the one who will fulfil My purpose in you[89] and I am the one who will cause you to prosper in everything to which you turn your hand.[90] Be humble, turn to Me, obey My word and I will cause you to fulfil all that I require of you.[91]

Psalm Twenty-two

AUTHOR *Lord, will You share with me about Psalm 22. I want to understand something of what You went through to get me saved.*

Psalm 22:1

AUTHOR *Why did You cry out, 'My God, My God, why have You forsaken Me?'*

JESUS You can have no conception of what was involved here. It is impossible for you to understand or comprehend the issues involved, but I will give you some insight at a level you can understand. When I was in the garden of Gethsemene praying to My Father for the cup to pass from Me it was because I had some awareness of what was to come.[1] As God, the Word,[2] I knew before I came what would be involved but as the Son of Man, in My human body I only had a partial awareness and understanding for I chose to set aside My own divinity[3] and to rely on the Holy Spirit for knowledge and understanding.[4] So I had some awareness of what was coming but I was not fully aware of everything that it would mean. I wanted the cup to pass from Me, not because of the physical pain that was coming, but because of the separation from My Father. I knew that if I took the sin of the world upon Me; that is, your sin, then this would inevitably cause Me to be separated from My Father.[5] Now you cannot possibly understand what this meant to Me for you have not had the relationship with the Father that I have. You were born separated from Him. You have never known what it is to be one with Him. Even though you have been reborn[6] and are now joined to Him[7] you still cannot appreciate My position. The Father and I are One. The Holy Spirit and I are One.[8] We have always been One from before the foundation of the world.[9] We have always been One. Always! Before time and outside of time. We are, and I am.[10] My very being, both as the Word and as the Son of Man, exists in the Father. To be separated means that My very existence ceases to be. By that I do not mean that I cease to be, for I am a Spirit and I am eternal (as are you), but that the very essence of My being ceases to be. It is difficult for Me to put it into words that you will understand; but I want to try and get over to you how utterly One We are and how breaking that unity and oneness would affect Me. But it is impossible for Me to do this for you have no frame of reference. Even your relationship, renewed as it is, with the Father can give you no true understanding of what it would mean for Me to be separated from Him and from the Spirit. It would be like entering a black hole where the whole of My being, My spirit and My very essence, would be sucked in and away from all that is light. There is no return from a black hole without a miracle intervention by the Father. Once something enters a black hole it is lost forever. Whole planets and stars can be swallowed up and their light extinguished. There is tremendous pressure in a black hole that just crushes everything and there is no escape. That is the nearest I can describe it. So when I was on the cross and I took your sin upon Me this is what started to happen. This is what I was dreading in the garden. This is what caused Me to sweat drops of blood.[11] This is why I cried out for another way even though I knew there was no other way.[12] So when I took hold of your sin,[13] as the Father laid it on Me, I began to feel Myself, that is My spirit, being drawn towards this black hole from which I knew there was no escape unless the Father intervened. I began to feel almost a panic come upon Me as I felt the presence of My Father, and the presence of the Spirit begin to recede from Me. I was being drawn away from Them, pulled faster and faster, and further and further from Their presence. I was moving further and further from the source of all light into the source of all blackness.[14] I could hear in My spirit the demons of hell calling for Me and laughing at Me as I was pulled faster and faster towards this black hole where Satan lives. It was in this moment that I felt totally alone. You cannot conceive how that felt for you have not experienced the perfect unity that We have. In that moment I felt the Father's love withdraw from Me. I felt His peace, His presence, His life sustaining presence[15] withdraw from Me and I began hurtling towards this black hole that is death – separation from the Father forever.

People do not understand what death is or they would flee from it with everything in their being. They do not understand the awfulness of separation from the Father's love forever, for they have never experienced it. People are born into separation so they have no concept of what it is like to be one with the Father and in His loving presence. Adam is the only one who understood. Not one of you can understand what it was like for Me to feel His love and presence recede from Me. It was this that caused Me to cry out to Him, 'My God, My God, why have You forsaken Me?'[16] There is an utter desperation and desolation in that cry, that will be echoed by millions of people when the day of judgement comes and they recognise that they have had the opportunity presented to them to experience unity with the Father and that they have turned it down. Why, oh why, My people, do you turn down the Father's love? You do not understand what you are doing. Listen to My messengers. Listen and respond to Me. Do not allow Satan to pull you into his black hole. You do not have to go there. You do not have to experience what I have experienced for you. For Me there was an escape. I knew My Father would bring Me out again for I was only to taste death on your behalf,[17] but for you there will be no escape if you reject Me now.[18] Listen to My messengers. Listen and believe, for they tell you the truth. Do not believe the lie. Hell is real. I know for I have been there and experienced it for you. Do not choose it for yourself. You have no understanding of what you are doing. Only believe. It is so simple, so straight forward. Come into My kingdom whilst there is still time. Do not turn away from Me but let Me rescue you from the black hole that is death, that is, separation from My Father's love and presence forever. My people, I do not want to hear you cry as I cried, 'My God, My God, why have You forsaken Me?', because for you there is no return. So turn now before you are drawn into that black hole. Turn now and be drawn towards the light. I am the light.[19] Come to Me and I will bring you into the presence of My Father[20] where you will experience His love and all that is good, all that is pure and beautiful forever. The choice is yours My people.[21] Life or death. Choose life. Choose life! Oh choose life and be with Me forever in the presence of My Father.

AUTHOR *Lord, why did it seem that the Father was so far from helping You?*

JESUS As the Son of Man, from the moment I was conceived, the Father has been there to help Me. All I had to do was call on Him and the Holy Spirit was there at My side to help and strengthen Me. When I was in the wilderness the Father sent the angels to minister to Me.[22] When I was in the garden of Gethsemene I said to Peter, 'Do you not know that I could call on the Father and He will send twelve legions of angels to rescue Me?'[23] Even on the cross I could have called on Him and He would have rescued Me, right up to the moment that I took your sin upon Me. The moment I became sin for you was the moment I started to be drawn towards that black hole. At that moment the Father and the Spirit began to withdraw from Me. At that moment I realised that for the first time ever I could not call on the Father for help. Your sin had put a barrier between Us that was impenetrable. It was as though My cry hit a brick wall. There was for the first time no response from heaven. There was a silence and an emptiness and a sense of aloneness that I had never ever experienced. The heavens were as brass. I felt utterly and desperately alone. There was no help there for Me. I experienced what you experience. I understood what you experience – except that you don't understand what you are experiencing for you do not understand the Father's love until you are born again. Then you begin to get a glimmer of understanding. To have known the Father as I have known Him and then to be cut off from Him is the most horrendous experience it is possible to have. It is impossible for Me to express to you the sense of utter desolation and despair and horror that came upon Me at that moment, even though I knew that at the appointed time He would reach down and pull Me from the pit.[24] Oh I wish I could make people understand what hell is like, what it is like to be separated from the Father's love. The tragedy is that so many of you are going to experience what I experienced. When you are called before the Father for judgement[25] you will at that moment understand His love and compassion and see the glory of His presence, and then you will be cut off from it and banished for ever into that black hole that swallows up your spirit.[26] Remember, My people, that this is not the end of your existence for you are spirits and you are eternal. This separation will be forever. There is no turning back; there is no rescue, for the Father cannot help you there. So turn now before it is too late. Turn now. There is help at hand now. The

Father is not far from you now. Indeed He is close at hand. He is only a call away.[27] One call for help is all that it takes for Him to come to your rescue and bring you into His kingdom. Call on the name of the Lord and you shall be saved. He is straining His ear listening for your call. Call now. Choose now. Make Me your Lord now and you need never experience what I experienced on the cross on your behalf. Why will you not believe? Why will you not call? What is keeping you from the perfect love of My Father, that you would choose the alternative? Open your blind eyes and see. Open your deaf ears and hear. Now is the day of salvation.[28] Not tomorrow, for tomorrow may be too late. Today the Father is not far from helping you. Today He is near and at hand. The word is in your heart, the word is in your mouth. All you have to do is speak it. All you have to do is call out and He will be there for you. The choice is yours. Choose life today.

AUTHOR *Lord, what are the words of Your groaning?*

JESUS The realisation that I was cut off from the Father's love and His presence, as the horror and blackness engulfed Me, produced in My spirit a groan so deep and so awful that words cannot express it. It was from the very core of My being and it expressed – I can't describe what it expressed. Words cannot describe what I felt at that moment as the sin of the world fell on My shoulders. I know that My Father heard that groan, and I know that it broke His heart at that moment for He was powerless to help Me, for We had agreed to do this so that you could be saved.[29] What really breaks His heart is when you reject what We have done and you still choose death over life, for there is nothing that He can do about that. He has done all He can by sacrificing Me on your behalf and I have done all I can by taking your sin. It is now up to each one of you how you respond to our love. We can do no more. The choice is yours.

Psalm 22:2

AUTHOR *Lord, why do You cry in the day time and in the night season and why does the Father not hear You?*

JESUS As I have said to you, today is the day of salvation. If you will cry out to the Father today He will hear you. When I became sin for you, that sin became a barrier between Me and My Father.[30] He could no longer hear My cry. Call out to Him today while He can still hear you, for if you reject the salvation that is offered to you today then that sin of yours will again become a barrier. You see, I took your sin and paid the penalty for it. When I had paid for it by taking it upon Myself it was removed far from you.[31] I offered you My righteousness in the place of your sin.[32] This opened the door to heaven so that when you call on the name of the Lord He will hear you and accept you into His kingdom.[33] But the day is coming soon when the age of grace will be closed and the time for all things to be finished will be here. If you have rejected the offer of salvation whilst it is still day then, when the time for the consummation of all things is come,[34] it will be as though you have taken your sin back onto yourself. You will have handed Me back My robe of righteousness that would have gained you entry into heaven,[35] and have put back on your cloak of sin. At that time the barrier between you and the Father will be reinstated and it will be forever. No longer will you be able to cry to the Father and have Him hear you. You can cry in the day and you can cry in the night but it will not make any difference, for He will not hear you, for the time for salvation will have passed and the time for judgement will have come. By your own actions and decision you will have set your destiny and there is nothing that you, or I, or the Father can do about it at that time. You will have sealed your own fate by rejecting the salvation that was so dearly bought for you. You will cry and you will cry and not be silent; for eternity you will cry but He will not hear. I know what this is like for I suffered this for a season when I became sin for you. Believe Me, you do not want to suffer this. Why, oh why would you choose to suffer so? Why will you not choose salvation today? Why, oh why will you not cry out to Him today whilst He can still hear you? It makes no sense. The enemy has blinded your eyes and deafened your ears[36] and you look and do not see and you listen but do not hear.[37] Open your eyes and open your ears and believe. There is more than enough evidence to prove that what My servants tell you is the truth. Believe what they say and cry out to the Father today whilst there is still time and whilst He can still hear you. Please do not reject Me. Please do not reject the Father. You do not understand how this grieves Us. But more than that, you do not understand the consequences of your actions. You do not understand what it is like to cry in the day time, and in the night season, and not be silent, when He cannot hear you. You do not know what the night season means. You do not understand what it means to be separated from the Father forever. But I do know, and I do understand, and I say to you again; do not do it, do not reject Me. Only believe and cry out to Him today, and He will hear you.

Psalm 22:3

AUTHOR *Lord, what do You mean by saying that the Father is holy and inhabits the praises of Israel?*

JESUS The Father is holy. The angels around the throne cry, 'Holy, holy, holy is the Lord God Almighty'.[38] They cry this continually as they are astounded again and again by the glory of His presence and being. You do not understand and can have no real conception of who the Father is and what He is like. He is so far removed from anything on earth that it is impossible to describe to you His power, His authority, His majesty, His awesome presence. He is so pure that the most pure gold on earth is as dross in comparison. His character is so pure that the holiest person on earth is evil in comparison. You are struggling to write this because you have no understanding, no comparison to make. Read the scriptures in Isaiah, Ezekiel and Revelation,[39] for those are the best descriptions that I can give you. There is no way that I can describe the love, the purity, the awesome power and the holiness of the Father to you. But I want you to realise who you are. You were created in His image. Even though you have fallen so far from perfection you are still created in His image. You are awesome beings. There is nothing in all of creation like you. But you fell far below even Satan, but I came to lift you up and raise you far above all principalities and powers.[40] I came that you might be restored to your former glory. My death on the cross was to accomplish this. And you are so precious to Us that We deemed it necessary to do this. You are so precious to Us that We did not want to lose you; you who were created in Our image. Therefore I agreed with the Father that I would go through death and separation for you so that you could return into fellowship with the Father. He is glorious and holy and when I have finished with those of you who respond to Me, you too will be glorious and holy.[41] You will not of course be on His level but you will be a reflection of Him. You will again be in His image. This is the purpose of the cross, to make it possible for you to be restored to your former glory. But as I have said before, if you reject this salvation there is nothing further We can do for you. You cannot come into His presence in your present condition. Unless you are restored to holiness you must be banished from His presence forever. And you can only be restored by coming to Me. I am the only one who has died in your place. I am the only one who has been raised again and I am the only one who has the power to lift you up alongside Me and restore you to your former glory. You must come to Me to be restored for there is no other name given under heaven by which you can be saved.[42]

AUTHOR *Lord, what about You inhabiting the praises of Israel?*

JESUS Israel is God's special people and you, the gentile

church, have been grafted into them.[43] As My people praise Me, and praise the Father, they build a place for Us to inhabit. They build a throne that We can sit on. Worship creates an environment that enables Us to visit with you. Your worship and your praise enable Us to meet with you. Our presence can dwell with you in an atmosphere of praise and worship. We love your praise and worship for it enables us to meet with you and to be with you. Through your praise and worship you build a habitation, a dwelling place, for Us to live. Solomon built a temple for the Father to dwell in, but, how can you build a building that is big enough for Me, says the Lord, that can contain Me? You cannot, for the earth is My footstool.[44] But you can do it in the Spirit, for the Spirit is not bound by time and space. In the Spirit you can build a dwelling place for Me to live.[45] It can be in each one of you individually, or corporately as you worship Me together. Wherever and whenever you worship Me I will be there with you enjoying your love and your fellowship. So keep on worshipping Me, says the Father, for I inhabit the praises of My people.

Psalm 22:4–5

AUTHOR *Lord, why did You talk about the Father being trustworthy to deliver Your forefathers?*

JESUS The Father is utterly trustworthy. You can rely on Him one hundred percent to perform His word. What He has said, He will do.[46] There is no shadow of turning in Him.[47] I knew that He was utterly trustworthy and that He would rescue Me from

Satan's black hole. If I had not been one hundred percent sure of this I could not have done what I did. That is why I cried, 'Into Your hands I commit My spirit'.[48] Even though I felt as though He abandoned Me and I went through and experienced all that you experience in death, I knew that there was the promise that He would lift Me back up to be with Him. I knew that He would not fail Me in this and it was this certain knowledge that enabled Me to entrust Myself to Him in this. I want you to know and understand, My people, the faithfulness of your Father. He will never leave you or forsake you.[49] It is you that leaves and forsakes Him. He never left Israel. Even though He was angry with them He never abandoned them and He never will. He is a God of covenant and He will not break covenant.[50] Especially will He not break the covenant which is sealed in My blood.[51] Covenant is unbreakable. You must get a revelation of this to understand the Father. He has laid down in His word the terms of that covenant and if you will fulfil your part of the covenant then He will fulfil His part. You must understand that many of the promises in that covenant are conditional. If you will fulfil the conditions then He will fulfil His part. But if you will not fulfil the conditions then He cannot fulfil the promise. And the conditions are not hard to fulfil for He has sent the Holy Spirit to you to give you the power and ability to fulfil those conditions. It is a matter of your will to fulfil them and not of your ability. But be assured that His word is sure and He is faithful to do what He has said He will do in His word. He delivered Israel as He said that He would.

He delivered Me from the grave as He said that He would and He will deliver you also if indeed you will turn to Him and call on His name.

Psalm 22:6

AUTHOR *Lord, what do You mean by saying that You were a worm and no man, and a reproach of men and despised of the people?*

JESUS I existed before the world was made. There is nothing made that I didn't make. I created Lucifer and all the angels. I created the heavens. I created the earth and all that is in it. It was all created by Me and for Me.[52] I am the Word that the Father spoke and sent forth. Everything that I created was pure, holy and of good report. It was very good, until iniquity was found in Lucifer. When he fell he was cast down low, far below My supreme creation – man.[53] But you, My beautiful people, bowed the knee to him and became the lowest of the low, and you corrupted the whole of the creation by your sin.[54] What was I to do? There was only one thing I could do. I left My place in heaven beside the Father and became as one of you,[55] except that I was not corrupted by your sin. Yet My people did not recognise Me. They did not know who I was, even though the Spirit had foretold My coming through the prophets.[56] Finally, as I hung on that cross, I took your sin upon Myself. In doing so I placed Myself into Satan's hands. I subjected Myself to him for a season. But My people did not understand what I was doing. In their pride and arrogance they thought that they were superior to Me. They looked only on the outside and did not understand the scriptures that explained what I was doing. As I became sin for them, and for you, they turned away from Me. They thought that I was no-one, worse than a common criminal, worse than them. In a sense they were right, for as I carried their sin, as I became sin for them, I was the lowest of the low. That sin weighed heavily on Me and pressed Me down, down, down. Satan thought that he was My lord and gloated over Me. As he was manifested in the religious leaders he mocked Me and he scoffed at Me and he despised Me.[57] He used the people to achieve his purpose and he used the voice of the people to express himself. He thought that he was lord over the whole earth, the whole of My creation, and finally, lord over Me. But if he had understood, if the people had understood, they would not have crucified the Lord of all glory.[58] But then My purposes would not have been achieved and you would still be in your sin, so I allowed Myself, indeed deliberately made Myself as a worm and no man, so that I could bring you up with Me when the Father lifted Me up again. I was as a helicopter winch man carrying out a rescue. The winch man allows himself to be lowered into the sea, or into the pit, so that he can take hold of the victim. Then when the winch man is lifted back up he can carry the victim with him back up to the helicopter. That is what I did for you. I allowed Myself to be scorned, to be despised and rejected so that I could be lowered into the pit of hell and the sea of the dead, so that I could take hold of you, and as the Father lifted Me back up to be with Him, I was able to carry you with Me, so that now you are seated with

Me in heavenly places.[59] I am no longer a worm. I am no longer a no-man. I am no longer a reproach and despised by the people. I am the Lord of all glory, honoured and respected by My Father, by all those in heaven, and by those on the earth who have understanding.[60] And you My people are seated in that place with Me as My bride. I am the only one who is worthy to open the scroll for I am the Lamb that was slain for you. I am the one who accomplished the rescue and I am honoured by My Father. And you, because you are Mine and I have clothed you with My righteousness, are worthy also – worthy to be My bride and to rule and reign with Me on this earth, for I snatched back from Satan control of My creation. It is Mine once more and the keys of death and of Hades are in My pocket.[61] The day is soon coming when the whole of the world will stand in awe of Me as I rule and reign over what is rightly Mine, and the knowledge of the glory of the Lord will be known throughout this earth.

Psalm 22:7–8

AUTHOR *What was it like for You to have all those people mocking You?*

JESUS They said, 'He trusted in the Lord, let Him rescue Him, let Him deliver Him, since He delights in Him'. You see, that was My strength, and it is yours too, that I did indeed trust in the Father. They thought to mock Me by saying this, but it was the truth. I had absolute and utter confidence in the Father. It was because of this that I was able to go to the cross. They did not understand. They did not believe that the Father could rescue Me, but I knew with absolute certainty that He could – right up to the moment that I became sin for you. Right up to that moment I knew that I could still call on Him and He would take Me down from the cross. And even beyond that I knew that He would rescue Me from the pit of hell, so their mocking did not bother Me. I knew they did not understand. I knew that this was something We had decided to do even before the foundation of the world, and I knew My Father would rescue Me at the appointed time, so their mocking was of no concern to Me. You too can have utter confidence in your Father and when trials and tribulations come your way, as they surely will, you too can have no fear of scorn or ridicule. You too, will be strong in testing for you too know the end from the beginning, for I have revealed it to you.[62] So do not fret yourselves over evil doers.[63] Their end is in My hands, as is yours. Just keep your eyes fixed on Me, the author and finisher of your faith,[64] and bless those who persecute you for they do not understand what they are doing.[65]

Psalm 22:9–10

JESUS I know My Father. I knew Him from before the foundation of the earth. I still knew Him at My conception for I was the same Word before and after My conception. Even though I set aside My own divinity[66] I still knew the Father. As the Son of Man I knew Him. In the womb I knew Him; from My birth I knew Him. Even though, as the Son of Man, I knew

Him as He was revealed to Me by the Holy Spirit, I still knew Him. He never left Me and Our relationship was continuous all My life. I was in constant communion with Him[67] and in this was My strength and My power. Your strength and power come from the same source and in the same way. As you commune with the Father through the Spirit who dwells within you, you too can know Him intimately. This is Our plan for you, this is Our intention, that you can have this same relationship with the Father as I had as Jesus the Son of Man. I do not say you will have the same knowledge of Him and relationship to Him as I have as the Word of God, but you can on the same level as I had as a human being, filled with the same Spirit. The same Father that is My God is your God also and you can trust in Him as I trusted in Him during My life on earth.

Psalm 22:11

AUTHOR *Lord, talk to me about this verse. Why did You say, 'Be not far from Me for trouble is near and there is none to help'?*

JESUS As I have already explained, the Father and I are One and We have always been together. When your sin separated Me from Him it was the cry of My heart that He be not far from Me. Even though there was now an impenetrable barrier between Us I knew that He was not in reality far away. Even though the separation was inevitable, I knew He would come for Me and rescue me at the appointed time. But at this moment, when I took your sin upon Myself, the door was opened for Satan. The way was open for him to attack Me. He and his demons had been waiting for this moment and trouble was near. I could sense this in My spirit as the moment for taking your sin drew near. This was what Satan was waiting for, for Me to become vulnerable to him. I was on My own, temporarily at his mercy, and there was no one who could help Me. I was the only one in all of creation who could do this for you and I felt very alone, even though I knew the Father was standing by to rescue Me as soon as My work was complete.

Psalm 22:12–13

AUTHOR *What do You mean by many bulls surrounding You, gaping at You with their mouths as a raging and roaring lion?*

JESUS Satan is the roaring lion seeking whom he may devour.[68] Now he has no teeth and he can only devour you if you let him. But then he was at the height of his power and the undefeated prince of this world.[69] He and his demonic hordes, the bulls of Bashan, were closing in for the kill. He sensed total victory, over Me and the Father. He sensed that he would soon own forever the title deed to this earth,[70] and as the Roman soldiers and the religious leaders of My people submitted themselves to him, they roared like lions and bayed like hyenas and pawed the ground like bulls as they anticipated destroying Me, the only hope for mankind. Had they succeeded in doing so there would have been no hope for you. You would have spent eternity in the power of Satan and separated from My Father. If Satan had managed to get Me to sin Myself during My life on earth I too would have been lost.[71] It was only by the power of the Holy Spirit dwelling within Me that I was able to withstand him and remain spotless, to be the perfect Lamb of God that could be sacrificed to take away your sin.[72] And by the grace of God I was able to do this, and so, even though the lions roared and the bulls encircled Me they could not destroy Me. So let them roar, for although I felt the terror, and their hot breath upon Me, I knew that they could not destroy Me. I knew that We had planned Satan's defeat. I knew that I was about to vanquish him forever, lead him in triumphal procession[73] and take his keys,[74] his authority in this earth, from him.[75] I have indeed won this victory and you now can be more than conquerors,[76] for I have given you My name and authority to step on scorpions and snakes[77] and to rebuke the devourer. He can no longer touch you, if you will stay close to Me and obedient to My word. The same Holy Spirit lives in you, and the same grace of God abounds towards you, to enable you to walk in the victory that I have won so dearly for you.

Psalm 22:14

AUTHOR *Lord, what do You mean when You say that You are poured out like water?*

JESUS I am poured out as a drink offering on the altar of sacrifice.[78] All My strength, all My life, all My being is poured out for you.[79] I was emptied of all that was within Me so that you could be filled. As the Holy

Spirit left Me it was as though I was totally emptied and poured out. There was nothing but an empty vessel left. This was so that you could be filled full to overflowing with the new wine of My kingdom, with the new wine of My love and with the new wine of the Spirit. And now I want you to do likewise, to pour yourselves out for others. Paul did this and he said that he left this world empty, poured out like a drink offering.[80] If you will do this I will refill you. As fast as you pour yourselves out for others I will refill you. You will never be empty for I fill empty vessels. As long as the widow had an empty vessel I filled it. I only stopped when I ran out of empty vessels, not when I ran out of oil.[81] My supply is inexhaustible and is only limited by a lack of empty vessels. So keep pouring yourselves out for others and I will continue to refill you. As I poured Myself out for you, you must do likewise for each other.

AUTHOR *Lord, what do You mean by Your bones being out of joint and Your heart being like wax melted within You?*

JESUS This is the effect of crucifixion. Dislocation of the joints occurs and the heart feels like it is melted within you. All your strength and all your being feels as though it is draining away from you, as though you are being poured out.

Psalm 22:15

AUTHOR *Lord, what does it mean by 'Your strength being dried up like a potsherd and Your tongue clinging to Your jaws?'*

JESUS I am poured out! I am poured out! All that is within Me has been poured out. There is nothing left to give. I have done all I can in this body. I have run the race and I have finished it. It is completed. It is done.[82] All that is necessary for Me to do to accomplish your salvation is done. My life has been poured out for you. There is nothing left to give. I have been brought to the point of death. It is time for Me to leave this body and enter Satan's domain where I will complete the task and establish the victory. My Father has brought Me to this point and now I am glad, for it is done.

Psalm 22:16–18

JESUS The dogs of Satan, the bulls of Bashan, have surrounded Me like vultures waiting for the final breath of life to ebb away and then they will swoop. They have pierced My hands and My feet. My bones stand out. They stand and stare but they have no comprehension of what they have done. They have no understanding that this was done for them and for you; that this was planned from before the beginning of time. All they see is one more wretched human being suffering in shame. And they mock and they scorn – except for one thief and one Roman soldier who have a flash of revelation.[83] But My people, the religious leaders of My people, have no understanding at all. Their minds are blank, devoid of revelation. Religion will do this to you My people. It will stop revelation. You must have revelation. Seek revelation, for My church is founded upon the revelation that I am the Christ, the Anointed One, and that I have been sent in the name of the Father to establish My kingdom on this earth.[84] If only they had known, if only Satan had known, he would not have crucified the Lord of all glory.[85] But he did not know and now Our plan can be fulfilled, for although they have circled around Me and are waiting for Me to die, they do not understand that at this moment I will have the victory, for death cannot hold Me. It has no sting for Me and now it has no sting for you, if you are in Me.[86] Understand My people, receive revelation My people, for I have the victory. The triumph is complete and Satan and his forces are defeated forever. Receive revelation My people and know who you are in Me, for I have conquered death and the grave and I have risen victorious, with the keys of death and Hades in My hand.

Psalm 22:19

AUTHOR *Why do You say, 'O Lord do not be far from Me?'*

JESUS At this moment of death I am totally alone. As I have described to you it was as though I was being swept towards a black hole from which there would be no escape, except that the Father rescue Me. Even though I was cut off from Him by your sin I knew He would not be far away. Now I can do nothing for Myself and I rely entirely on Him. He is My strength and My salvation, as He is yours.[87] He is My hope, just as He is yours.[88] So rely on Him as I relied on Him. Cry out to Him as I cried out to Him and He will save you from your black hole as He saved Me from Mine. I cried out to Him and He answered Me.[89] He will answer you also. He will! For He is utterly trustworthy and His arm is stretched forth to save.[90] Cry out to Him. Call upon His name and He will save you too. There is no need for you to suffer death. All it takes for you to escape is that you cry out to Him, and then He will answer you. He will respond to you and He will lift you out of the miry clay.[91] He will reach down into that black hole and pull you up into His marvellous light.[92] Just one call. Just one cry and He will come. Why will you not call? Why will you not cry out? The choice is yours My people, the choice is yours. I have done My part. I have made it possible. Now you must do your part, and choose. Life or death; you choose.[93] But know that apart from Me there is no salvation, for I am the only one who has suffered death in your place. I am the only one who was raised from the dead and it is only by coming to Me that you can participate in the life that exists in Me,[94] for I am the resurrection and the life.[95] There is no other name given to men by which they can be saved.[96] So come to Me and I will take you into the presence of the Father of lights,[97] who loves you so much that He gave His only Son so that whosoever should believe on Him should not die but have eternal life.[98] And that life is knowing My Father[99] and His love forever.

Psalm 22:20–21

AUTHOR *Lord, why do You say, 'deliver Me from the sword, My precious life from the power of the dog, and from the lion's mouth and the horns of the wild oxen?'*

JESUS My life is precious to Me and My life is precious to you. My life is precious to Me for it is the only life I have and yet I was prepared to give up that life for you. I was prepared to lay it down for you because,[100] first and foremost, I love the Father and I desired to do His will above My own. If that was what He desired from Me because of His love for you, then that was My desire also. My only desire is to please the Father and have Him say to Me, 'You are My Son in whom I am well pleased'.[101] Let this desire be in you also, that you please the Father. I only did what He told Me to do, and I only said what He told Me to say, for I am totally submitted to Him out of My love for Him. Do you love the Father as I do? Are you submitted to Him out of love?[102] This is how it should be. Your only desire should be to do the Father's will, for out of that comes great blessing.[103] So, My life was precious to Me but I was prepared to lay it down for you. But My life was also precious to you, and it was essential for your sakes that the Father rescue Me from the lion's mouth and from the power of the dog. Had the Father not rescued Me I would have been lost forever. And if I was lost forever then you also would have been lost forever. Therefore I cried out to Him for your sakes, that He rescue Me and deliver Me from the sword. Your life depends on My life, for you are dead in your trespasses and sins apart from Me.[104] It is no longer you who live but I who live in you.[105] Your life is hidden in Me.[106] Without Me you have no life, for without Me you have no forgiveness of sin. You are dead apart from Me. It is not you who lives but I that live in you and through you. Therefore I cried out to the Father that He deliver Me so that you could live. And He heard Me! Out of His holy hill He heard Me and He answered Me.[107] With mighty power He reached down from heaven and lifted Me up from the depths of the earth and placed Me beside Him in heavenly places, where I sit at His right hand in glorious victory.[108] And because you are in Me then you too sit at His right hand in glorious victory. The lion, the dog, the wild oxen, Satan himself, have no power over you any longer, provided you remain in Me and it is My life that is lived in you and through you, for you and I are one, and you are hidden in Me, clothed in My righteousness. We have achieved what We set out to do, the Father and I, and by the mighty power of the Spirit it has been accomplished and Satan has been defeated for ever, and you have been rescued forever, for no one and no thing can snatch you out of Our presence again.[109] My joy is complete for My creation has been restored to Me and we have fellowship once again, you and I.

Psalm 22:22

AUTHOR *Who are Your brethren, Lord, and in what way will You declare the Father's name to them?*

JESUS I have both natural brethren and spiritual brethren. My natural brethren are the Jewish people – My brethren according to the flesh. It was always My intention and purpose to come first to My natural brethren.[110] Salvation was first to be made available to them.[111] Through them salvation would come to the gentile church.[112] But first and foremost I came to declare to the Jewish people, My people, what the Father was really like and what His purpose was. To the Jews were given the revelation through the written word, through Moses, through the psalms and all the prophets. My people were given the plan for the salvation of all mankind.[113] They were Our covenant people through whom I would have legal entry into the world as a human being. My purpose was to show the Father to them in His true light for they had a very distorted view of Him and did not understand His nature, His character or His purposes. So I came to declare His name to My people even though many of the religious leaders would not have ears to hear. I stood in the midst of the congregation, in the synagogues, and in the temple and gave praise to the Father's name. Those who listened were given understanding and revelation. They understood and they turned to Him. When I return I will again glorify the name of My Father. Again I will stand in the midst of the congregation of the whole earth and declare to the world who the Father is. I have not finished with My natural brethren yet.[114] The day is coming when the veil will be removed from their eyes, and they will look on Him whom they pierced and they will mourn and they will understand.[115] But grace will be available to them, and salvation will be available to them, and they will repent and turn to their Father who will forgive them and re-establish His covenant with them forever, and they will indeed be His people and He their God. But I also have brethren in the Spirit. I am the firstborn from the dead,[116] and all of you who are born from above are My brethren, for we all have the same Father, and I will declare the name of the Father to you. I will give Him praise and declare to you what He has done, for the Spirit will take what I say and declare it to you.[117] I will give you revelation and understanding of who the Father really is and what is His heart towards you who believe. In the midst of the congregation I will show you the heart of the Father, how much He loves you, how much He cares for you and how He longs to spend time with His children. His heart is towards you and not against you. His heart is to bless you and not to curse you. He is your ever loving Father who longs for fellowship with His children. His heart is to see you healed, restored, prosperous and successful in all that you do. You are precious in His sight and He loves you. Yes, I will declare this to you by My Spirit in the midst of the congregation. Listen to what the Spirit is saying to the church and receive the Father's love.

Psalm 22:23

AUTHOR *What does it mean to fear the Lord and to praise Him?*

JESUS To fear the Lord is to honour and respect Him. It is to understand who He is. This understanding can only come by revelation. This is the work of the Holy Spirit, to give you revelation of the Father. When you begin to understand His awesome power, and the holiness of His nature, your natural reaction will be to fear Him. I do not mean that you should be afraid of Him, for with understanding of who He is should also come understanding of His loving-kindness towards you. To fear Him is to give Him honour and respect. To give Him honour and respect is to obey Him. You cannot say that you love the Father, that you honour the Father, and not do what He tells you to do. To fear the Lord is to be obedient to His word. And if you fear Him you will want to give Him praise. To have any understanding of Him is to want to give thanks to Him for what He has done for you by praising His name. That is, to tell others of what he has done for you. As the Father has blessed you by lifting you out of the miry clay and placing you in heavenly places beside Him, you will want to tell others of this and glorify the Father's name to them so that they too can turn to Him. The knowledge of the Lord is to be known throughout the earth, and it can only be so as you, My brothers, declare and praise His name to those who do not yet know Him. This is what He wants you to do and if you fear Him, love and respect Him, you will do His will.

AUTHOR *Who are the descendants of Jacob and the offspring of Israel who will glorify Him?*

JESUS Those who will glorify Him are those who know Him. You cannot glorify the Father and praise His name unless you know Him. True worship and true praise come out of a living relationship with the Father.[118] No one who does not have this relationship can truly praise Him, and only those who are born of His Spirit can have such a relationship with Him. Having a relationship with Him is not the same as knowing about Him.[119] Who are the descendants of Jacob? The descendants of Jacob, and the children of Israel, are those who know Him. Abraham was their father. Abraham knew His God. Abraham had a relationship with the Father for there was covenant between them. The offspring of Abraham are those who fear the Lord, who obey His word and have covenant relationship with Him. They are those who are born from above and are circumcised of heart.[120] They shall know their God and out of that intimate relationship will come the honour, the fear, the love and the respect. Understanding of His true nature will also come to them and they will glorify His name throughout the earth.

Psalm 22:24

AUTHOR *What is the true nature of the Father?*

JESUS The Father is love.[121] He loves you with an everlasting love. His love is boundless and without measure. His love is as vast as the ocean and as deep as the sea. You can never out run, or run out of the Father's love for you. It is His love for you that motivated Him to send Me to be afflicted in your place, and it is My love for you that caused Me to be afflicted for you, for the Father and I are One. He has not despised nor abhorred the affliction of the afflicted nor has He hidden His face from him. He has never turned away from you and His face has always been towards you. As the father of the prodigal son waited day after day, searching the horizon for a glimpse of his lost son, so the Father has searched for you.[122] He has not turned His face from you but searches diligently for you. His eyes roam the whole earth searching for those whose heart is towards Him so that He might show Himself strong on your behalf.[123] No, He has not abhorred your affliction nor turned His face from you. It is you, My people, who have turned away from Him. It is you who have erected a barrier of sin between you and the Father. This is not His doing; it is yours. He longs to tear down that barrier and to resume fellowship with you but He must wait for you to return to Him. Just as the father of the prodigal had to wait for his son to return so does your Father have to wait for you. But when you cry out to Him He will hear you, for His ear is strained to catch the sound of your voice. It does not matter how far away you are, how afflicted you have become, or what you may have done, for His ear is strained to hear you the moment you cry out to Him. The moment you cry out, however faint or however weak that cry might be, He will hear you and draw you back to Himself. No, He has not despised you nor abhorred you, for He has despised and rejected Me in your place.[124] He has hated Me so that He could continue to love you. And He does love you and longs to hear your voice cry out to Him. He will hear you, for He is listening for your cry and His eyes are searching the whole earth to find you and bring you back into fellowship with Him and into His everlasting and wondrous love.

Psalm 22:25

AUTHOR *Lord, who is the great congregation and what are the vows that You will pay before those who fear the Father, and who are they?*

JESUS To praise someone is to give thanks to them for what they have done. To give thanks to someone is to praise their name. In other words it is to make their name known to others, to tell others of what they have done. I made a vow to My Father that I would make His name known throughout the earth. There are so many people that do not know Him, that do not even know of Him. How can He be their ever-loving Father when they do not know of Him? How can He have fellowship with His children when they do not know He exists? Even though We have built into man a consciousness that there is a Creator, by the world We have created,[125] so many have pushed this consciousness so far down through the glorification of the intellect[126] that they are unable to relate at all to a merciful and loving Creator. So I made a vow to My Father that I would make His name known throughout this earth. I made a vow that I would tell the world of all the wondrous things He has done in the earth. But even more than what He has done in creating the earth and in creating you, I vowed I would tell the world what He was like. I said that I would go to the earth and reveal His true nature to His people. This is why I said to Philip, 'If you have seen Me then you have seen the Father, for I and the Father are One'.[127] I came to show you the Father, to reveal His heart to you, so that you would know that He loves you with an everlasting love and that He desires to save you from the consequences of your sin, and to bring you back into fellowship with Him forever. I have performed My vow in front of the whole world, the great congregation. My death was the payment of My vow, for as I was lifted up I drew the whole world to Me,[128] and as they come to Me I bring them to the Father, for no one can come to the

Father except by Me and My death on the cross.[129] And now My people, I need to continue to pay My vow to give praise to His name in the great congregation. But I am now in heaven seated at His right hand, so how can I continue to pay My vow? You My people, you who know Me, are My body on this earth. You are My mouth, My hands and My feet. Enable Me to pay My vow and go throughout this earth and tell of all the marvellous things that your Father has done for you, of how He restored you and brought you back into fellowship with Him, and how you rest in His ever-loving arms. Go My people, go. The time is short. I am with you, My Spirit is in you. Go throughout the earth and declare to the world the praises of Him who brought you out of darkness and into His marvellous light,[130] and those who fear His name will hear you and turn to Him and He shall save them too.

Psalm 22:26

AUTHOR *Why will the poor eat and be satisfied, and why will those who seek You praise the Lord? What does it mean by, 'Let your heart live forever'?*

JESUS The poor are those who hunger and thirst after righteousness.[131] They will be blessed for they will be filled and satisfied. As you go throughout the earth declaring the praise of the Father you will awaken in some people a thirst and a hunger for righteousness. This world is dying of starvation of the spirit. There is no word, there is no prophet, there is no light, but darkness only, and My people are desperate for light. Gross darkness is covering the earth and people do not know where to turn.[132] But My glory is rising upon the church and the Sun of Righteousness is rising with healing in His wings.[133] As My church shines with My glory those who are hungering and thirsting after righteousness will know to whom to turn to be filled and satisfied, for you will tell them of Me and I will lead them to the Father who is the source of all supply. As they come to Him their needs will be met and they will be filled. I am the true bread and whoever eats of Me will never hunger again.[134] I am the true water and whoever drinks of Me will never thirst again,[135] for I will provide bread for the hungry and rivers of living water for the thirsty that will flow out of the belly becoming a never-drying fountain within them. Their joy will be complete as they feed on Me. Ho! Everyone who thirsts, come to the waters and drink freely. Come, buy bread without money and be satisfied, you who are hungry, and I will supply your needs.[136] This world cannot satisfy, this world cannot supply your needs, but only My Father in heaven. So seek Him you hungry and you who are thirsty. Seek the Father and you will be satisfied. Praise His name amongst the congregation, My church, so that the poor of spirit will know where to find salvation. Let your heart live forever My people. Do not be deceived; life can only be found in the One who is the source of that life. I am the resurrection and I am the life.[137] No one comes to the Father but through Me for I am the source of all life. Let your heart live, let your spirit live, feed on Me, drink of My life-giving Spirit and come to Me, My people, and I will supply your need. I will satisfy your hunger and quench your thirst for righteousness.

Come to Me and buy food and drink that is eternal and which truly satisfies. Then indeed you will praise the Lord.

Psalm 22:27–28

AUTHOR *What will all the ends of the world remember and why will all the families of the nations worship before You?*

JESUS The ends of the world will remember that there is a God in heaven. I have built into each one of you a knowledge of Me. It is hidden in the deepest part of you but it is there. There is a fundamental and basic instinct in each of you that knows there is a Creator, and that is why I have said to you that you are without excuse, because the creation speaks of Me. But many of you have pushed that memory so far down that you can no longer remember that it is I who created you. By exalting your own feeble intellect to the place of god in your lives you have suppressed your God given memory of Me to the point that you no longer admit that it exists. But you shall remember Me, for I am going to bring it to the foreground of your minds. I am going to force you to acknowledge that there is a God in heaven as My glory rises upon My church and they perform signs and wonders in My name that can have no other explanation but that I have done them. The knowledge of Me will spread throughout this earth and every one of you will be forced to make your choice. Will you serve Me or will you serve your enemy and master, the devil? I will set you free but he will destroy you. Choose Me and choose life. Do not choose death, but choose you must, one or the other.

Be wise and turn to Me for I am coming to reclaim My earth and I will rule forever. There will be a separation such as has never been before. Those who have chosen Satan will be banished from the earth forever and will spend eternity with the lord of their choice in hell.[138] Those who choose life now, before I come, will live forever with their Lord on the earth in My glorious kingdom of life and light.[139] Darkness or light, death or life, you choose, but choose you must and choose you will before I come to claim My inheritance. All those who choose life will come and worship the Father. All the families of the earth will come before Him and bow down to Him for they will desire to worship Him, their Creator. Yes, the whole earth will be filled with the knowledge of the Lord and all will worship Him, for the kingdom, the power and the glory are His and His kingdom will have no end.[140]

Psalm 22:29

AUTHOR *Who are the prosperous of the earth and why will they eat and worship?*

JESUS The prosperous of the earth shall be those who inherit the earth. The meek and the lowly are those who inherit the earth,[141] and they are the ones who have submitted themselves in this age to the authority of My word. Those who have recognised Me as Lord and invited Me to be their Lord, now in this age, will inherit the earth when I return to take up My kingdom and My throne. They will rule and reign with Me in the next age and forever. They will inherit the kingdom that My Father has prepared for them before the foundation of the world. They shall be prosperous indeed, for that has always been Our intention for you. We want you to have abundance and to rejoice in Us. This will be so in the new age to come, but you can indeed enter into that prosperity, that peace, that shalom, now in this age, where there is nothing broken and nothing missing in your lives, where everything is well with you. You who are called by My name shall indeed be prosperous in My kingdom and you will eat and you will be satisfied and you will worship the Father indeed, forever.

AUTHOR *Who are those who go down to the dust and why will they bow before You? Why can't they keep themselves alive?*

JESUS Those who go down to the dust are those who die. I am not talking about the death of the body but the death of the spirit. It is impossible for a man to keep himself spiritually alive for you are all born in sin and in spiritual death. You are all separated from the Father and there is no way that you can make yourselves spiritually alive again. If that were possible then there would have been no need for Me to come and pay the price for your sin.[142] There would have been no need for Me to suffer death on your behalf. It is only because I died and was raised up again that you can be raised up in Me to be with the Father, for it is no longer you who lives but I who live in you and through you by My Spirit. It is only the energising power of the Spirit dwelling in you that causes you to live.[143] That same mighty power that raised Me from death raises you also.[144] It is that power, that life of the Father – eternal life – that causes you to live now. So a man cannot keep himself alive and without Me must go down to the dust. That man will be separated from Me and from the Father and His life-giving Spirit forever. But as I have said to you before, that is not the end of that man's existence, for you are spirits and you are eternal beings. You cannot cease to exist and you will exist forever. Will you exist forever in Me, in eternal life, or will you exist forever outside of Me in eternal death? The choice is yours, but know this, that every knee will bow to Me and every tongue will confess that I am Lord.[145] Every human being, every spirit, every thing that has been created, was created through Me and for Me and will bow the knee to Me. Will you not bow the knee to Me now freely, out of your own choice and your own will, for the benefits are literally out of this world? Will you not choose now, in this age, to make Me your Lord so that I can love you and have fellowship with you in My Father's kingdom? Why will you wait until you are forced to bow the knee to Me along with your current lord and master, that fallen creation, Lucifer? Why on earth would you choose him over Me? I cannot understand, except that he has blinded your eyes and deceived you, and you will not listen to those that I have sent to you to reveal to you the truth.[146] Listen to them, believe their report and make Me your Lord now before the day that judgement comes. For judgement is surely coming on this wicked and unrepentant generation that will not listen to Me or to My servants. Do not be one of those who go down to the dust, but be one of those who are the prosperous of the earth, those who will inherit the kingdom that My Father has prepared for them from before the foundation of the earth. I am Lord! Choose Me as your Lord now before it is too late, before you go to the dust, before the end of this present age. For I am Lord and you will bow the knee to Me sooner or later, one way or the other. But make it sooner, make it now and make it your choice, for I long for you to be in My kingdom and I do not want to lose you forever.[147] But I have given you the freedom to make that choice and I will not take that freedom away from you. You are free to choose, but you are not free to escape the consequences of that choice, so choose wisely and choose Me today before it is too late, for today is the day of salvation. Call on My name today and you will be saved, you will enter into My kingdom and you will be with Me forever this day.

Psalm 22:30–31

AUTHOR *Lord, what do You mean by, 'a posterity shall serve Him' and that, 'it will be recounted of the Lord to the next generation?'*

JESUS After the separation of the sheep from the goats there will be a remnant who will enter My kingdom.[148] This remnant will serve Me in My kingdom and I will bless them abundantly. They will be My inheritance, the people whom I have saved from the black hole of death. During My reign of one thousand years, before I hand the kingdom back to My Father[149] when all things are made new,[150] there will be many more generations born who will not have experienced this present age. They will have no understanding of the devastation that Satan caused during his reign of terror. They will have no knowledge of him and what he did, for he will be shut up in his prison during this time.[151] You, My people, who have survived into this new age, must recount to those about to be born what the Lord has done for you and how He rescued you. No longer will My people tell of how the Lord brought His people up from Egypt into the promised land, but they will tell of how the Lord has brought His people from the 'egypt' of this world system into the promised land of His kingdom on earth. Tell this to the people who will be born during the next thousand years, declare to them the righteous ways of the Lord so that they will know how He has delivered His people from the fires of hell.[152] My people will need to know this for Satan is only in prison for a little while. At the end of the one thousand years he must be let out to deceive the people again.[153] Make sure that the future generations know of him so that they are not deceived. Make sure that they know of what the Lord has done for mankind so that they will know to resist the evil one as he attempts to deceive the world again; before his final rebellion and his destruction in the everlasting fire, along with all those who chose him as lord in this present age. Yes, there will be a posterity who will serve Me, a people who will delight to do My will and to seek My face. Blessed are those who will inherit this earth for they shall see the kingdom of God and shall live in His righteous and glorious presence all their days.[154] They shall not see death, they shall not fear that black hole, for I have won the victory over death and it has lost its sting for them.[155] Yes, My people, I have accomplished what I set out to do. I have a bride, and My Father has a family. We have a posterity that will love Us, obey Us and delight to be in Our presence. And We, the Father, the Spirit and I, will delight in you and We shall make Our home with you on the earth forever.[156]

Psalm Twenty-three

Psalm 23:1

AUTHOR *What does it mean for You to be my shepherd? What is a shepherd?*

JESUS The shepherd is the protector of the flock. The shepherd is the provider for the flock. The sheep are totally at the mercy of the shepherd and they trust him perfectly. He is the one who leads them. He is the one who walks before them. He is the one who goes into every situation before the sheep go there. He is the one who defends them against attacks by wild animals. He is the one who defends them against the attacks of thieves and robbers. He is the one who sees to their every need, who rescues them when they stray, who binds their wounds when they fall. He is the one who leads them to green pastures and beside still waters. He is the one that the sheep implicitly trust. He is the one who knows the way. He is the one who plans where they are going. All the sheep have to do is follow the leading of the shepherd. The sheep have no other responsibility, and no other concern, than to listen to the voice of the shepherd and to go wherever he goes. If they will do this they will have no need to worry or be concerned. They will have no need to worry about food or drink for all those things are the responsibility of the shepherd and not the sheep. The good shepherd will lay down his life for the sheep if that should become necessary. I am the Good Shepherd and I have lain down My life for My sheep. But I have taken it up again and need never lay it down again.[1] I have taken it up and I will continue to lead My sheep. My sheep know My voice and they will follow Me wherever I go. That is all I require of you. Listen for My voice, obey My voice and follow Me. If you will do this you will never get lost and you will find that all your needs are met.[2] I am your provider and I will lead you to the green pastures and the still waters. I will provide for all your needs and I will protect you from those who would attack you. No weapon formed against you shall prosper for that is your heritage as one of My sheep.[3] Keep following Me. Keep listening to My voice and all will be well, for I know where we are going. I have a plan and a purpose for you[4] and I know the destination and I know the way. There is no need for you to know this. There is no need for you to worry about this, for I know and I am leading you. You will not go astray if you stay within the sound of My voice.[5] You know My voice for you are My sheep and you learn to recognise My voice as you spend time in My presence. I am your Shepherd. You shall not want and you shall not lack any good thing.

Psalm 23:2

AUTHOR *Why do You make us lie down in green pastures?*

JESUS Sometimes I have to make My sheep lie down for My sheep are not always sensible. My sheep will just keep going and going until they drop from exhaustion. Therefore I have to insist that they lie down and rest. You were not designed to keep going without a rest. Even I rested on the seventh day.[6] There is a time for work and a time for rest.[7] You ignore the time for rest at your peril. It is a disease and a lie of this world that efficiency comes from going faster and faster and doing more and more. This is not so. Efficiency comes through obeying My word and My word says you must rest. Therefore I will make My sheep lie down and rest. The green pastures are where they feed and recoup from the journey. Green pastures are rich nourishing food. You need to take time to feed on My word and to digest My word. You digest My word by meditating on it, chewing it over in your mind as a cow chews the cud. Speak it to yourself.[8] Ask the Holy Spirit for revelation and He will give it.[9] You must take this time or you will starve to death. You take time out every day to feed your natural body. You must do the same with your spirit. So lie down in the green pastures and eat. This is wisdom and essential. It is My plan for you to do this. I do not want you to keep going and going, faster and faster. This is the enemy's plan to destroy you and burn you out. Listen to Me and stop and rest, and feed on My word in the green pastures.

AUTHOR *What about the still waters?*

JESUS The still waters speak of My Spirit. In stillness is your strength,[10] for when you are still you can hear My voice. Be still and know that I am God.[11] As you wait on Me your strength is renewed.[12] So come aside and lie beside the still waters. Calm yourselves, still your minds and allow yourselves the opportunity to listen to what My Spirit is saying to you. How can you hear My voice if you won't stand still long enough? You cannot hear Me amid all the hustle and bustle. So come aside and listen. It is essential that you do this for how will you know where I am leading you if you cannot hear My voice? The sheep that go astray are the ones that don't lie down when I stop. They keep going and wander off. Do not be like that. When I lead you beside the still waters and into the green pastures then stop and rest. Listen to what I want to say to you by My Spirit[13] and feed on My word. You must do this, and as a good shepherd who is concerned for his sheep I will make you do this.

Psalm 23:3

AUTHOR *What do You mean by restoring my soul?*

JESUS Your soul is your mind, will and emotions. As you go through life your soul becomes contaminated by the world. You become weary of well-doing,[14] you become battered by the storms of life. Your mind is filled with the rubbish of the world. Your emotions are pulled this way and that. It is necessary for you to come aside to restore your peace and equilibrium. As you rest in the green pastures and beside the still waters, as you fix your mind on Me and rest in My presence, I am able to restore and replenish your soul. Your mind is renewed as you study My word,[15] your emotions are restored as you look to Me as the author and finisher of your faith,[16] and your will is restored as you listen to My voice directing you. I am the solid rock on which to build your life,[17] and as you go through the storms of life you will find refreshing and restoration, and a new infilling and a new purpose as you focus on Me. As you lie beside the river and drink from the water of the Holy Spirit your vitality and zest for life will be restored.

AUTHOR *You lead me in the paths of righteousness for Your name's sake.*

JESUS My purpose is to lead you to a specific place, and that is to be beside Me forever as My bride.[18] You can follow Me for you know where I am going and you know how to get there, for I am the way.[19] If you stick close to Me, walking where I walk and going where I go, then I will lead you to that place.[20] Do not stray or go your own way. Be obedient to My voice as expressed in My word and by the Spirit within you. Keep in close fellowship with Me so that you are within the sound of My voice. Do not allow the world to crowd out My voice with its noise.[21] Keep coming back to the still waters and the green pastures so that I can restore your soul. Stop when I say to stop and come aside when I say to rest. Do not be so busy that you do not have time for this, for there is nothing more important than the time you spend resting in My presence. If you do not stop and rest you will not be able to hear My voice, and if you cannot hear My voice then you will go astray, for you will wander off on your own. If this happens I will come and find you,[22] for it is for My sake that I want you with Me, for you are My bride. But it would be much better if you stuck close to Me at all times for then I can lead you in the paths of righteousness and we can arrive at our destination together. Being together is our destination. This is My purpose for you, that we will be together forever as husband and wife. This is why it is so important to Me that you allow Me to lead you in the paths of righteousness, for I am coming for a bride who is perfect and without spot or wrinkle.[23] The way of righteousness is narrow and difficult and not many find it.[24] That is why you must stay within the sound of My voice so that I can direct you and say, 'This is the way. Walk in it'.[25] As My body on this earth you carry My name and for My name's sake I want you to walk a righteous path so that those who look at you will see Me and desire to follow Me also. I have conferred on you great honour and privilege by allowing you to represent Me in this earth. Do not abuse that privilege but bring honour and glory to My name as you walk the paths of righteousness.

Psalm 23:4

AUTHOR *What is the valley of the shadow of death and why will I fear no evil?*

JESUS The ultimate weapon that the enemy has against people is death. His desire is to separate people from Me forever, for that is his fate.[26] He died when he rose up against Me and attempted to lift himself higher than My throne.[27] But the result of that rebellion was death. That is, he was cast out of My presence forever[28] and will live out his existence in the lake of fire in perpetual death, which is separation from Me forever. In revenge he wants to take as many people with him as possible, and to My great distress and sorrow many will choose to go with him. He has blinded their eyes[29] and they cannot see what death means – separation from Me and My love forever. But you, My children who have been born of My Spirit, cannot taste true death for you have already passed from death to life.[30] Yes your bodies will die, but that is not true death. That is only stepping from this world into My glorious presence. You, My children, will never taste true death for nothing can separate you from My love and from My presence, for you have chosen to be with Me now. Death then for you is only a shadow. The most the enemy can threaten you with is a shadow of death. He cannot touch you with the real thing because I tasted the real thing on your behalf[31] and I conquered death. Death has lost its sting for you, for you are alive in Me forever more.[32] So if death casts a shadow over you and you have to walk through the valley, remember that you are walking through the valley. However deep the valley seems to be, however dark and gloomy it is, remember that you are walking through and you will come out the other side into My glorious presence. Persecutions may come, evil may come and cast its shadow on you for a while, but it cannot ultimately touch you for it is only a shadow. Therefore you will have no fear of evil. Even if you are called to die for Me you will not fear this, for you know that it is only a shadow and the shadow will flee away in the light of My presence. Therefore fear no evil for I am with you. I have already walked this path. I have tasted and conquered the real thing and death cannot touch you for you can never be separated from My presence and My love.[33] I am with you all the way. I walk beside you all the time and however dark and gloomy the valley may seem, keep your eyes fixed on Me and remember that it is only a shadow.

AUTHOR *What are Your rod and Your staff that comfort me?*

JESUS I am the rod from the stem of Jesse.[34] I am your rod and your staff. The rod was a weapon with which the shepherd defended the sheep against attack by the wild animals, and the staff was a support that he leaned on. I am your rod and your staff. I am the word, and the word is both your support and your weapon. You are to lean on My word at all times. It will comfort you and support you in times of trouble. My word will never fail you or let you down. Lean on My word and trust My word. My word is sure and it is truth, for I am truth.[35] When the shadow of death hovers over you hold fast to the promises in My word. Take hold of that truth and rely on it to support you as you go through the valley. Trust My word, trust Me, at all times and it will not fail you. My word must be in your hand. That is, you must take hold of My word by meditating upon it,[36] by renewing your mind with it[37] so that it dwells richly within you.[38] Only when you know My word can it fully support you. If you do not study My word and put it into your mind, and in your spirit, it is like having a staff that is lying on the ground. It cannot support you whilst it is on the ground. You must take hold of it in your hand. You take hold of My word by reading it, speaking it, studying it and meditating it. Get it into your being. Make it part of you. Study it day and night. Do not let go of it and then it will support you in times of trouble. The purpose of the rod was to be a weapon against attack by wild animals. In the valley of the shadow of death wild animals will attack you. I know, for they attacked Me. The strong bulls of Bashan encircled Me and gaped at Me with their mouths. Dogs surrounded Me and the assembly of the wicked enclosed Me.[39] When Satan attacks you then you will need My rod, My word. Use your sword[40] and declare, 'It is written'![41] They will not be able to harm you as you fend them off with My word. Again, your staff and your rod must be in your hand. They are no good lying on the ground. So take them up. Take up My word and use it and it will comfort you, it will support you and it will protect you at all times. For I am My word and I am with you in the valley of the shadow of death.

Psalm 23:5

AUTHOR *What is the table You prepare before me in the presence of my enemies and who are my enemies?*

JESUS Your enemies are two-fold. First and foremost your enemy is Satan, and the spiritual powers in high places and the demonic hordes.[42] Satan seeks to destroy you and bring you down, but he cannot succeed for I am with you and you shall have good success in whatever you put your hand to.[43] Secondly, your enemies are those who have given themselves over into Satan's control. He will use people, sometimes people in the church, to stand against you and oppose you. Do not be surprised at this. Most opposition comes from those who claim to be Mine but are still in bondage to religion. Satan can very easily influence them for he is a master of religion. However, you must remember not to fight the people but to fight the one who is using them. He is your true enemy and not the people themselves. But even though they come against you I will prepare a table for you. I have much to give you. I have an abundance of food and drink that I want to give you. It will be very obvious to your enemies that I am blessing you,[44] and that I am abundantly providing for you and supplying all your need.[45] I will justify you in the sight of your enemies and they will know that I am with you.[46] The food that I will give you is My word[47] and the drink that I will give you is the Holy Spirit.[48] Eat abundantly and drink abundantly in the presence of your enemies that you may be strong and filled with living water. There will be much else on the table for you besides the food and drink. The table speaks of My provision and I will supply all your need. As you supply the needs of others out of what you now have, you will be able to come to the table I have prepared for you and take whatever you need,[49] both for yourself and to continue to supply the needs of those who are not yet My children. I will supply your need. You supply their need, and that will make it clear to them that there is a God in heaven and that He cares for them.[50] Your enemies will see this and be ashamed for they will know that I am with you and that I am blessing you.

AUTHOR *You anoint my head with oil and my cup runs over?*

JESUS The oil speaks of the Holy Spirit and the anointing speaks of Me empowering you to accomplish what I have called you to do.[51] As the oil is poured over your head it speaks of your mind being renewed and submitted to Me, so that you have the mind of the Anointed One.[52] You need the anointing of the Holy Spirit. You need His power and ability to do what I have called you to do. I do not expect you to accomplish anything in your own strength and in your own ability.[53] What I have called you to do I will also empower you to do. I will anoint you abundantly with the Holy Spirit and He will enable you to complete what I have given you to do. Ask for the anointing. Keep asking.[54] Keep being filled. As you give out keep being refilled. Ask and you will receive, for I need you to be filled continually so that you can do what I have called you to do. You cannot be a blessing to others if you are not filled yourself. So seek the anointing. Seize every opportunity to receive more and more and more. I will fill you up to overflowing so that there will be abundance, and that overflow will affect all those you come into contact with. It was not Peter's shadow that healed the sick but the anointing that was flowing from him.[55] I want you to be overflowing with that anointing oil so that those you come into contact with will also receive. Do not seek just enough for yourself. Seek to overflow into the world around you, for it is the anointing that breaks the yoke of bondage that is upon them.[56] You will see them set free just because they have been in your presence. It is the overflow of the anointing that is on you that will accomplish this.

You are containers of the anointing oil that will set My people free. Seek to be filled to overflowing and seek to take that overflow into the world that so desperately needs Me.

Psalm 23:6

AUTHOR *Lord, what does it mean for goodness and mercy to follow me? What is goodness?*

FATHER Goodness is all that I am. Do you remember – Moses asked to see My glory and I said that I would make all My goodness pass before him.[57] Goodness is all that I am, the weight of My glory and My splendour. My goodness is everything that is perfect and right. Only good gifts come from Me for I don't possess anything else.[58] Goodness is Me.

AUTHOR *What is mercy?*

FATHER Mercy is My loving kindness towards you. Mercy is what I extend to you in the place of judgement. Judgement is what you deserve. Death is what you deserve.[59] You deserve to be separated from My goodness forever. But loving kindness is what I give to you instead. Mercy is what I give to you instead. In My mercy I judged My Son in your place so that you could experience My goodness,[60] so that you could be in My presence forever. I still seek to extend goodness and mercy to you all the days of your life. For I love you and I want to be with you and to see you prosper and have good success in all that you do. If you will obey My word and seek My face as Moses did then I will cause My goodness to pass before you. Indeed if you will seek My face with all your heart I will cause My goodness and My mercy to follow you all the days of your life. Indeed they will not only follow you but they will run after you and chase you until they catch you and overtake you.[61] My goodness and My mercy will seek you out to bless you and cause you to prosper – if you will do My word and seek My face. And, My child, I want you to treat your brothers and sisters in the same way. I want you to extend goodness and mercy to them also. I want you to pray blessing on them also. As you are filled with My goodness and My mercy let it overflow to those around you so that they too can receive from Me through you. If you will do this then goodness and mercy will indeed follow you all the days of your life.

AUTHOR *How will I dwell in Your house forever?*

FATHER My child, it is My purpose and My plan that you will always be in My presence. This was My intention from before the foundation of the world, that we would dwell together. You will be My people and I will be your God and we will dwell together on the earth forever. Did I not walk in the garden with Adam? Satan has sought to destroy the fellowship between us but he has not succeeded for My Son was worthy and He has restored all things. When all is completed we will indeed walk together again and I will make My dwelling on the earth with men.[62] Indeed I have made you even now My dwelling place for I dwell in you by My Spirit.[63] You are My dwelling place, and My dwelling place will be with men on the new earth.[64] You will indeed dwell in the house of the Lord forever. The fellowship between Me and My creation will never be broken again, for there will be no hurt or harm in My holy hill.[65] There will be no death or destruction there, for the former things will be no more.[66] When everything is completed those who have sought Me will indeed dwell with Me forever.

Psalm Twenty-four

Psalm 24:1

AUTHOR *Lord, You said that You have given the earth to men, but now You are saying that it is Yours and all its fullness, and all who dwell in it.*

JESUS Yes, I did give the earth to men to be their domain.[1] I gave them dominion over it as I have dominion in heaven.[2] But I only leased the earth to men. I still retain ownership of it, for I created it. I gave it into your hands for you to look after on My behalf. I gave it to you to rule and reign over for Me, for that is what I created you to do. But you gave My earth and all its fullness away to My enemy.[3] You even gave yourselves away. But I have bought the earth back. With My blood I bought it back. I bought the earth back, all its fullness back, and I bought you back.[4] I have redeemed you and you are Mine. I have set My stamp of ownership upon you by sealing you with My Spirit.[5] And now I have sent you again to rule and reign on the earth on My behalf until I come.[6] But when I come, and it will be soon, your lease will be up and I will take control of My earth again.[7] As the Son of Man I will rule and reign here on this earth and you will assist Me until I hand all things back to My Father and your Father. So, yes indeed the earth and all its fullness, including you, does belong to our Father and He rejoices in it and He rejoices in you, His children.

Psalm 24:2

AUTHOR *Lord, what do You mean by saying that You founded the earth upon the seas and established it upon the waters?*

FATHER I created the earth to be a blessing to My people. I created abundance and not lack. I built into the earth a system that with proper care would never produce lack or shortage. I created out of the seas a land that was fertile and good. Even the seas themselves were teeming with life and with food for you. I established this earth in prosperity and abundance. As the flooding Nile brings prosperity to Egypt so I have built prosperity into this earth. I created abundance, not lack. If you would obey My word and come to Me there would be no shortage. It is only because you have turned from Me and gone your own selfish ways that the rains are withheld and the seas run dry.[8] Turn back to Me and I will heal the land and restore the abundance to the seas.[9] Turn back to Me and let Me provide for you again. What I created was good, it was plentiful, it was abundant prosperity, but you thought that you knew better than I and you turned, each of you, to your own ways and to your own wisdom.[10] Look around you and see what you have done to My creation that I gave you. Turn back to Me and I will restore the abundance that I created. Indeed at the end of time, when all is completed and My Son hands the earth back to Me, I will indeed restore My creation to what it was at first. I will give you new heavens and a new earth for you to reign over under the supervision of My Servant Jesus.[11] And then indeed there will again be abundance. There will be no lack and the earth will again bring forth good things. It will again be established in prosperity on the flooding waters and all its fullness will be for you.

Psalm 24:3

AUTHOR *Lord, what is Your hill and Your holy place?*

FATHER My hill and My holy place are where I dwell, where My presence rests in this earth.[12] I have chosen Zion as My resting place in this earth, both the physical natural Zion and spiritual Zion. I chose, from before the foundation of the world, a place that I would meet with you and that place is in Jerusalem. Jerusalem is My city for it is the city of the Great King.[13] All down the ages I have chosen Zion as My resting place, ever since I gave Mt. Moriah to king David.[14] Indeed even before that, in the time of Abraham,[15] I established Jerusalem as the place that I would meet with you and meet your need.[16] It was in this place that I would supply your greatest need, your need for redemption, and there on My holy hill of Moriah I provided for you a sacrifice, the sacrifice of My Son, that would enable you to be restored to fellowship with Me. And so I have chosen Jerusalem as My city and it shall always be Mine. Even though men fight over it, it shall always be Mine and I will establish My King on His throne in that city very shortly, and He shall reign over the nations from there.[17] Jerusalem is the city that I love[18] and woe to anyone who comes against her.[19] My hand is on Jerusalem and I will not tolerate the nations desecrating her anymore. I have made her a cup of drunkenness to the nations and I will bring those who fight over her before her where I will destroy them,[20] for there shall not be hurt or harm in My holy city[21] when I establish My King on her throne. Woe to the nations who fight and squabble over her for your time is up. It is time for Me to establish My Righteousness in My holy city,[22] for Zion is My dwelling place on this earth. But I have another holy place on this earth where I dwell, and that holy place is in you My people,[23] you who are called by My name. In you I reside, and in you and through you I meet with the world in this age until My Son returns in person. You are My holy dwelling so allow Me to perfect holiness in you[24] as I dwell in you by My Spirit, for the people of the world are watching you to see if they can find Me in you, My church. Set a light on My holy hill[25] so that a light shall shine in the great darkness that covers the earth.[26] Let My light shine in you and from you as a beacon of My presence in this dark age. Let the people see Me in you, and let them come to Me through you, as My light shines from My holy hill, My dwelling place on this earth, that is, you My special people who are called by My name.[27]

Psalm 24:4

AUTHOR *Lord, who can ascend Your holy hill and stand in the holy place? What does it mean to have clean hands and a pure heart?*

FATHER Only those who are righteous and pure in My sight can ascend My hill and stand in the holy place. This is because nothing that is impure can survive in My presence. Only that which is pure and holy will remain in My refining fire.[28] My glory will burn up and destroy all impurities.[29] Therefore you must be totally and absolutely pure to stand in My presence. None of you are that. You have all sinned and fallen short of My glory[30] and therefore how could any of you stand in My presence or ascend My holy hill? You cannot. No, not one of you, for you are all imperfect. Who then can ascend My hill and stand in the holy place? You cannot, for you would be instantly destroyed. But there is a way, for I have created a way, that each one of you can come into My presence and stand in My glory. There is an answer to this problem. The answer is that you must die. You must die before you come into My presence. You must die, and then you must be raised up again. You must no longer come in your own unrighteousness, but you must come in the righteousness of My Son.[31] The solution is for you to be united with Him in His death as He paid for all your sin, and you must be united with Him in His resurrection so that you can live.[32] Indeed you must be hidden in Him,[33] so that when you come into My presence it will no longer be you who lives but Christ who lives in you, and your life must be hidden in Him. Then when you come into My presence you will be protected by His righteousness, and will not be trusting in your own. To attempt to come into My presence trusting in your own righteousness would mean instant death and destruction and there would be no resurrection for you. So you must choose to die now and join your life to that of My Son so that you can share in His resurrection. Then you can come into My presence, for it will no longer be you who lives, for you will be dead, but it will be Christ who lives in you, and in Him you will have clean hands and a pure heart for He will clothe you with His righteousness; and when I look on you I will see Him, and His righteousness will protect you from the consuming fire of My presence when you stand before Me in the holy place. So come to Him now, join yourselves to Him now, for there is no other way that you can ascend My holy hill and stand in My presence. There is no other way that you can have clean hands and a pure heart. Only in Him can you live and move and have your being.[34] Outside of Him lies only death and destruction, for He is the resurrection and the life.[35] So come to Him today, join yourself to Him today, and make Him your Lord today, for today is the day of salvation,[36] not tomorrow but today, for tomorrow may not come for you and then how would you enter My presence. You cannot, for you do not have a pure heart and you do not have clean hands, for all your righteousness is as filthy rags in My sight.[37] Only the righteousness of My Son Jesus can enable you to stand in My presence. Only He is the way of salvation for I have given no other name under heaven by which you can be saved.[38]

AUTHOR *Lord, what does it mean to lift up your soul to an idol and swear deceitfully?*

FATHER To lift up your soul to an idol is to put your trust for salvation in anyone, or any thing, other than in My precious Son Jesus who died for you. An idol is anything or anyone who takes a higher or more prominent place in your life than I do. To trust in an idol is to trust in anything that is false. To trust in an idol is pure folly for no idol can get you into heaven and into My presence. Anything that you trust in for your salvation other than the sacrifice that My Son made for you, His shed blood that removes your sin,[39] His resurrection life that allows you to live again and His righteousness that allows you to enter My presence, is a false hope and an idol. Religion is a false hope, whether it is the 'Christian' religion or any other, for religion is you trying to gain favour from Me by your own efforts.[40] As I have already explained, all your righteousness is as filthy rags in My sight. Your righteousness is dross and you will be consumed by My pure, holy and refining fire. You can only enter My presence, and therefore heaven, if you are clothed in the righteousness of My Son, for His righteousness will protect you, as a fire proof suit will protect a fireman as he enters the flames. To attempt to come into My presence by any other means than by trusting in My Son Jesus is folly and will lead to instant death for you and separation from Me forever.[41] So do not lift up your soul to an idol, for an idol cannot save you. I have laid down the way of salvation for you. Any other way is an idol and a false hope. Do not swear by any other method. Do not expect to come to Me in any other way than by making My Son Jesus your Lord and Saviour and putting your trust in Him, for in Him alone is forgiveness of sin and right standing with Me.[42]

Psalm 24:5

AUTHOR *Lord, what is the blessing that we receive when we trust in Jesus for our salvation?*

FATHER My son, when you come to Me trusting in the righteousness of My Son instead of your own righteousness, when you put your faith in His ability to save you instead of your own ability to save yourself, then you open the door for Me to bless you. I have for you such treasures and such delights that you have no idea of,[43] both in this life and in the next. My treasure house is opened to you the moment that you make Jesus your Lord. Because you are in Him everything that belongs to Him belongs to you. All that is His inheritance is your inheritance, for you are also My son.[44] And His inheritance is everything that there is, for everything that was made, was made by Him and for Him,[45] and because you are in Him it is all yours also. Do not underestimate what I have for you. But you will of course underestimate it because you do not have any understanding of the richness of your inheritance. You do not know what is laid up for you, what I have in store for you. Everything that My word says you can have is yours now in this life. You have only to learn how to appropriate it, to get it from heaven to earth. Pay attention to My word and I will teach you how to do this. Your salvation does not just get you a ticket into heaven but is a complete package that includes the righteousness of My Son,[46] the healing for your bodies that He bought,[47] the wholeness and well-being of your soul, the peace that passes understanding[48] and prosperity both in spirit and in the flesh. You see, My desire has always been to bless you for I am your loving heavenly Father. And just as you delight to bless your children and provide for their needs and see them prosper in every area of their lives so I desire to see you prosper and fulfil your potential. I am the God of blessing and not of cursing. Only good gifts come from Me, the Father of lights.[49] So turn to Me and let Me bless you with every spiritual blessing in heavenly places.[50] Let Me cause your soul to prosper so that you may be in health and prosper in all things.[51] I want to see every area of your lives blessed, both the spiritual and the physical, for I want to meet all your need, whatever it is.[52] I am not just concerned about your spiritual needs but about every aspect of your lives for you are My children and I love you so much. So if you will come to Jesus and give Him all your unrighteousness and allow Him to clothe you with His righteousness you will enter into the blessing that I have set aside for you this day.

Psalm 24:6

AUTHOR *Lord, what does verse six mean?*

JESUS Jacob is the father of the nation of Israel, My own special people. Because they are My own people I have chosen to bless them beyond all the nations of the world. If only they would turn back to Me and obey My word they would indeed be able to receive that blessing. But for now they are estranged from Me, but they shall return,[53] when they 'look on Him whom they pierced'[54] and say 'blessed is He who comes in the name of the Lord'.[55] Then their eyes shall be opened and they shall see again.[56] But in the meantime it is you who are the generation of Jacob for you do seek My face. You, the gentile church, have been grafted in to the rootstock of the Son of Jesse[57] and you shall partake of the blessing of Jacob until the time of the gentiles is completed and the blindness is removed from My people's eyes. You are indeed the generation of Jacob for you seek My face and you have become one with the nation of Israel, and if you will bless My people you too shall be blessed.[58] Yes, seek My face My people, seek first the kingdom and its righteousness and all the other things will be added to you.[59] Do not despise My people Israel for in Christ there is no gentile or Jew for you are all one,[60] and My people Israel will once again seek My face at the time appointed for them.

Psalm 24:7

AUTHOR *Lord, what do the gates and the doors represent, and what does it mean for them to be lifted up?*

FATHER The doors are the way in, and the gates are the structure in the wall that the doors fit into. The gate is where the council of elders sat to do the business of the city.[61] The gates represent My people, My elders. Lift up your heads My people and look around you. Do you not see that your King is coming to you, riding on a white horse?[62] Lift up your heads My people and prepare. Prepare you the way of the Lord. Make His path straight and get the people of the earth ready to receive Him.[63] Prepare yourselves, My people, for your King is coming to you. He is on His way and the time is short. Meet together you elders. Come together and take counsel of Me, for I will give you instruction and direction.[64] Lift up your heads O you gates, and seek Me. Seek My face. Seek My presence, seek My will, seek My counsel, seek Me. Oh seek Me, My people, for I am your Lord and your God. My ways are not your ways. My thoughts are not your thoughts,[65] so take counsel from Me and I will prepare you to receive your King. Open the doors, fling wide the gates and the King of Glory shall come in. Open the doors of your hearts, My people, fling wide the gates of your lives, My people, and let the King of Glory come in.[66] Behold He is coming to you riding on the clouds,[67] so lift high your heads and you will see Him. Lift high your heads and seek Me and I will direct you. Take counsel from Me and not from this world, for the counsel of this world will lead you astray.[68] Lift high your heads and keep your eyes fixed on Jesus, for He is the author and finisher of your faith.[69] He is your King, the King of Glory, and if you will prepare yourselves, prepare those around you, and prepare the way, He will come to you and enter into your lives and your hearts.

Psalm 24: 8–9

AUTHOR *Lord, who is the King of Glory? Why is He strong and mighty, mighty in battle?*

FATHER Jesus! Jesus is the King of Glory. He is the Great King. He is My King whom I will set on My holy hill to rule and reign over this earth forever.[70] He is the king of Glory. He is clothed in the glory of heaven. He carries all the weight and splendour of heaven and He is coming to you. No, He is not coming lowly and riding a donkey,[71] but He is coming in splendour riding on a white horse, and He has a name on His thigh, 'King of Kings and Lord of Lords'.[72] Yes He is coming to you mighty in battle, for He has defeated His enemy and your enemy, Satan.[73] He is coming with the armies of heaven to wreak havoc amongst those who have stood against Me. He is coming to execute My vengeance on all those who rebel against Me,[74] for the day of vengeance and justice is at hand for all those who have not accepted My offer of peace.[75] Those who are at enmity with Me shall know that I am God and that My Son reigns indeed. Yes, He is the Great King, the mighty warrior, victorious in battle, and who can stand against Him in the coming days. Lift high your heads O you gates and be lifted up you everlasting doors and the King of Glory will come to you. In victory, and in justice, and in righteousness He will come,[76] to execute My judgement upon this earth.[77] The time is short. Do you not recognise it? Do you not hear the sound of the armies of heaven preparing to come? Yes they are coming, so turn now, turn to Me and accept the peace terms that

I offer you. Accept My Son Jesus as your Lord today and He will come to you as your King, your Brother and your Saviour.

Psalm 24:10

AUTHOR *Lord, who is the King of Glory?*

FATHER The Lord of hosts, He is the King of Glory. I am the King of Glory for My Son and I are one. We reign on high. We command the hosts of heaven and We command the hosts of the earth.[78] My Son and I are one. He is My right arm and My strength.[79] He is the Mighty Power that holds the universe together.[80] He is My Word that I have sent forth into this world.[81] Obey My Word.[82] Obey My King and fall before Him in awe and wonder for He and I are one. I am Jehovah, the Self Existent and Eternal One,[83] the great I AM,[84] the LORD GOD.[85] Honour My Son and you honour Me.[86] Deny My Son and you deny Me.[87] I will not be denied for the earth will be filled with the knowledge of Me.[88] O you people, lift up your heads, open wide the everlasting doors for I am coming to you. In great wrath I am coming to you[89] for you have denied Me, and rejected and despised Me.[90] But no longer. I am coming to establish My Kingdom and My rule and I will set My King upon My holy hill. I will establish Him in the earth and I will laugh at all those who thought to scorn and mock Me.[91] But it is not too late. There is still a little time. The age of grace has not yet closed, so turn back to Me whilst there is still time. Turn back to Me and repent, you peoples of the earth. Listen to My witnesses whom I have sent to you.

Listen to them, repent and come back to Me,[92] and I will receive you into My kingdom as My friends and My sons.

Psalm Thirty-three

Psalm 33:1

AUTHOR *Lord, why should the righteous rejoice in You?*

FATHER Why should you not rejoice in Me, My people? When you consider what I have done for you does it not make you want to rejoice? Does it not make you want to shout out, spin around and be gleeful? I have rescued you from the miry clay, out of the dark pit and from the depths of hell. I have redeemed your life from destruction. I have placed your feet upon a solid rock.[1] I have given you new life – My life. I have given you My name. I have given you access to all that I have[2] and I have betrothed you to My Son[3] and seated you in heavenly places beside Me.[4] Does this not make you want to rejoice, My people? It should. What more could I do for you? I have showered you with heavenly blessings.[5] I have poured out My Spirit upon you.[6] I have made you new creatures in Christ.[7] I have made you My sons and My heirs.[8] Surely you will rejoice in Me? Surely you will give thanks to My name and tell others of what I have done for you and of what I can do for them? Rejoice My people, rejoice in

Me and give thanks to My name.[9] This is right and proper in My sight and it blesses Me greatly. Your praise and your thanks are beautiful in My ears. To see you rejoice in Me is beautiful in My sight. But it is not just so that I can be blessed that I command you to rejoice and give Me praise. And it is a command that you rejoice. I command you to rejoice at all times and in all circumstances because then I can still the enemy and the avenger on your behalf. He can have no control over you when you rejoice in Me in all circumstances. When he brings all manner of evil against you and persecutions abound, when he seeks to destroy you, how do you think he feels when all you do is rejoice the louder in Me? What can he do to you when you rejoice in every circumstance that he throws against you? He is totally devastated and defeated. He will leave you alone when all that he can do to you only causes you to rejoice in Me more. If when he tries to turn you against Me all you do is rejoice the more he will not continue his assault on you for it will be self-defeating for him. So rejoice in Me My people at all times and in all circumstances and bless your Father who loves you and rejoices in you too. Yes your praise is beautiful in My sight and beautiful in My ears, so rejoice again My people. I say again, rejoice![10]

Psalm 33:2–3

FATHER Praise Me with the harp. Sing to Me with a stringed instrument. Use the skills that I have given you to praise Me. I have given you these skills for a purpose. I have created you to be like Me.[11] Heaven is filled with music of all kinds.[12] Music is the instrument of praise and worship. I have given you the skill to create, to create instruments on which you can make a joyful noise to Me, and skill to play those instruments in a way that delights Me.[13] I have given you the skill to make melody that echoes the melodies of heaven.[14] I have given you new songs to sing,[15] songs that come from My Spirit directly into your spirit from the very throne-room of heaven and from the very heart of your God. Use what I have given you, My children, to rejoice in Me and praise Me. Your enemy Satan has taken and corrupted what I gave him and he has turned it against Me and against you.[16] Music is the very stuff of heaven. Music is the expression of My heart and of your heart. Listen to his music and you will know what is in the heart of a man. Listen to what he sings, listen to the music he enjoys and you will know the depths of his heart, for I created music to be the expression of what is in the depths of a man. But your enemy corrupted this wonderful gift and turned it to express the evil depths of his heart. So I want you, My people, to express what is in your hearts through the music you play and the songs that you sing. Let what is in your heart be what is in My heart and let My heart flow through you and out of you in the music that you make. Let it come from Me, flow through you and then back to Me in a cycle of blessing. As the rain falls from the heavens, cleanses the earth and returns to the heavens bringing refreshing and life, so let your music come from the heavens, flow through you cleansing and refreshing your souls, and let it pour forth from you and return to the heavens from whence it came and let it bring rejoicing both to you and to Me, for it is through music that our hearts are knit together and it is through music that we express our intimacy, you and I. So, My people, play and sing with all that is within you. Skilfully play the harp and the stringed instruments, the flute and the drum. Make a joyful noise unto Me and sing new songs of the Spirit as you praise My name and rejoice in Me. Let the world know what is in your heart as you worship Me, your Father and your God, and I will still the enemy and the avenger for your sake indeed.[17]

AUTHOR *Lord, what do You mean when You say that music is the very stuff of heaven?*

FATHER Heaven is the expression of Me. Heaven reflects all that I am. Heaven was created out of Me, that is, it is a manifestation of Me. As I speak I create what I say.[18] As I sing I express My heart, My very being. Music that comes forth from Me created heaven. Just as My Word went forth and created the earth, so My Word went forth from Me in song and created heaven. Heaven is therefore filled with Me. It is a manifestation of Me and it is created from and by the music and the Word that comes from Me. As the world is sustained by the Word of My power[19] so heaven is created and maintained by My Word, for everything was created by Him, through Him and for Him, for He is the expression of Me.[20] Music then is the very stuff from which heaven was created.

AUTHOR *Lord can You explain a bit more about the role of music?*

FATHER I have created music to be the vehicle through which I express Myself in the most intimate way. I have given you the same ability so that we can relate to each other in the same way. I have given you the power of speech so that you can express what is in your mind both to Me and to each other. But I have given you music so that you can express what is in your heart, for music goes much deeper than words. Through it you can express what is hidden deep within you, in the very essence of your being. Heaven is filled with music for I am constantly expressing My heart and the angels respond in like manner.[21] My intention was for the world to be filled with music and I created Lucifer to be the angel in charge of this, but corruption was found in him and he has corrupted the music of the earth so that now the earth is filled with violence and evil.[22] But you, My people, have been restored and My gift of music has been restored within you so that again you can express the depths of your being to Me and to each other. With words you can express your mind; with music you can express your souls. When you combine the words and the music your self expression is complete. But when you combine the words of the Spirit with the music of the Spirit then you can fully express what is in your spirit. This is the ultimate. This is why I delight when you sing in the Spirit, in melody and harmony that comes straight from My throne and straight from My heart, for then you express Me in you, and the intimacy of our relationship. That truly is a delight to Me. When you sing in the Spirit all of heaven stops what it is doing and joins in. Have you not heard the angels as they sing with you? Every ear is listening to the expression of our love for each other and our delight in each other. Therefore do not neglect the gift of music that I have given you for it is the most intimate expression of your love for Me, and of My love for you. It is heaven itself come on earth.

Psalm 33:4

AUTHOR *Lord, what do You mean by, 'the word of the Lord is right'?*

FATHER My word is righteous. There is nothing in My word that is not righteous. My word is equity, that is, it is full of truth and justice. It is My heart that righteousness is done on the earth. It is My heart that all men are treated fairly and equally. It is My heart that when you look at what was done and what was said in any situation that you should declare, 'Yes, that was just, that was proper, that was fair, that was done righteously'.[23] It is My heart that righteousness should abound on the earth for I hate injustice. Injustice comes from the enemy. There is no injustice in heaven for there is no injustice in Me. I always deal righteously and fairly in all things.[24] Therefore My word is right and My word is righteous, for My word expresses My heart. You can therefore rely on My word and make My word your standard and your plumb-line.[25] My word is right. My word is correct. It is just and true and all that I say and all that I do is truth and righteousness.[26]

Psalm 33:5

JESUS Yes, I love righteousness and justice. I hate injustice and unrighteousness and I will come against anyone who acts in an unrighteous and unjust manner against his brother.[27] When I come, the earth will be filled with equity as I rule in justice. Understand My heart and do likewise.[28] I hate injustice, I hate unfairness and I will come against anyone who oppresses, or treats his brother unfairly. When I come, the earth will be filled with My goodness, but for now you are My people in the earth and I expect you to act as I would act, and through you I will demonstrate My love for justice and righteousness, and in you will the world know and see My goodness in the earth.

Psalm 33:6

AUTHOR *Lord, how were the heavens made by the breath of Your mouth?*

FATHER The heavens were made by My word.[29] As have I already said, music is the stuff of heaven. Faith is the stuff out of which the heavens were created,[30] both the heaven where I live and the heavens that cover the earth. The stars were made from faith. As I conceive something in My heart I have faith that what I have conceived will come into being. I express My thoughts in words, and the breath of My mouth (My Spirit) sends these words forth.[31] My words are not void, they are not empty but they contain faith and from that faith is created that thing which I have conceived in My heart. No, My words are not empty, they are not void, but they accomplish what I say.[32] By the power of My Spirit I have what I say. And you, My people, are created in My image and I have said that what you believe in your heart and say with your mouth you shall have.[33] My word is powerful and active and does not return to Me void but accomplishes that which I have sent it to do. Do not underestimate the power of your words to accomplish what you say, for good or for evil. My words always produce good things for My heart is full of righteousness, but your hearts are not so.[34] Therefore be careful what you speak for you may not rejoice in what your words accomplish as they go forth from your mouth.

Psalm 33:7

AUTHOR *Lord, what do You mean by 'gathering the waters of the sea together as a heap and laying up the deep in storehouses'?*

FATHER The earth is Mine and the fullness thereof.[35] I have created the earth and I have formed the earth by the word that goes forth from My mouth. Not one part of the earth, or one aspect of the earth has been formed by chance. Everything has been positioned in its correct place by My word and everything is maintained in its place by My word.[36] The seas and the land were formed by Me and remain in their place by My word. The depths of the seas are a storehouse of riches which I have set aside for you. As long as you obey My word and turn to Me they will never run dry.[37] Do not think that chance or random selection plays any part in this for I have created the world and all its fullness for you. Yes, it belongs to Me, but I created it for you. I formed and fashioned it for you and I maintain it for you and I will restore it for you when I come again into My kingdom.[38]

Psalm 33:8–9

AUTHOR *Why should the inhabitants stand in awe of You?*

FATHER Do you not know who I AM?[39] If you truly knew Me you would fall on your faces in dread of Me. If you understood My power, if you understood My holiness, if you understood My glory then indeed you would fall on your faces in awe of Me.[40] I am the Most Holy God, the One and Only God Almighty. I am all powerful, all present and all knowing, and I know you, My people, each one of you intimately. If you knew the power of My word you would tremble at My voice. You would run from Me as did the children of Israel in fear and dread.[41] But if you knew Me, if you knew My character, if you knew how much I love you, if you knew how much I long to be with you, if you knew My mercy and My grace towards you, then you would run to Me and throw yourselves into My arms. If you truly knew Me you would fear Me and you would love Me and respect Me, and if you loved, respected and honoured Me as you should, then we could walk together as a Father and son should. For you are My offspring, you are My heirs and you are My children.[42] Yes, I have spoken – and it is so. What I say, I shall have, and I have declared that those of you who live on the earth, who have turned back to Me, shall be My children indeed and you shall inherit this earth that I have spoken into being just for you.[43] For this earth shall not fail, it shall not cease to be, for it is eternal,[44] for My word is eternal, and as long as My word goes forth, resounding around the universe, this earth shall remain for you.

Psalm 33:10

AUTHOR *Lord, how do You overcome the plans of the nations?*

FATHER The peoples and nations of the world plot a vain thing.[45] They take no account of Me in their plans, neither do they heed My word. I have set out in My word what I require of people. I have set out in My word what I intend to do, but the rulers of the nations choose to ignore Me as though I do not exist. However, I do exist and I will ensure that what I have said I will do shall come to pass.[46] As I have in the past, with Egypt[47] and with rebellious Israel,[48] I have used the wickedness of the leaders to further My plans and I will do so again now. You must remember that the rulers of this world are still being manipulated and used by My enemy Satan. Although people have a free will they are not fully free to exercise it. They believe they are making free choices but in reality they are not.[49] Just as Satan manipulates and controls people to get his will done in the earth, I can use peoples and situations to My advantage to fulfil My will in the earth, and Satan is no match for Me. So let the rulers of this world and the peoples of this age plan and plot as much as they want for I will bring their plans and their counsels to nought. I will frustrate the plans of the crafty[50] and through My own people, the church, I will ensure that My will is done on this earth as it is in heaven.[51]

Psalm 33:11

FATHER My counsel stands forever and the plans of My heart to all generations. It is a wise nation whose leaders seek counsel of Me and it is a prosperous people who follow the plans of My heart. I have written down in My book for you the plans of My heart and My purposes for the earth. Be a wise and understanding people and pray that the rulers of your nation will take heed of My word and seek counsel of Me, says your Lord.[52]

Psalm 33:12

FATHER I will abundantly bless the nations of the world who seek to do My will. Why do you think that the 'Christian' nations of this world are the nations that have been the most blessed? Why are some nations more advanced and more blessed than others? Look at their heritage; look at how they have related to Me and how they have received the gospel of My Son. Compare these nations with the poor nations of the world and check their heritage and see whom they have worshipped.[53] Yes, I have indeed blessed the nations that have founded themselves on My word and on My precepts. But sadly many of those nations have begun to turn from Me and their blessing is turning to cursing as they drift further and further away from My precepts. Turn back to Me O you foolish people and allow Me to restore to you the blessings that you once had. Blessed indeed is the nation whose God is the Lord. See how I have turned peoples and nations around as they have repented and turned to Me as their God. I can do this for you too if only you will repent as a people and turn back to Me. Humble yourselves and pray. Seek My face, turn from your wicked ways and I will hear from heaven and heal your land.[54] Pray for the leaders of your nation,[55] that they will fear Me and keep My word that you may be a wise and understanding people. If you will do this then I will choose you as My inheritance and you will be a blessed nation indeed.

Psalm 33:13–15

AUTHOR *Lord do You really watch what each one of us is doing all the time?*

FATHER Yes I do. I am intensely interested in what each one of you is doing. You are all so very precious to Me, even those of you who are rebellious and stiff-necked and who will have nothing to do with Me. Each one of you is so important to Me and I am sorely distressed when you will not turn to Me, and you insist on going your own way even to the point of going to hell. So, yes I do watch what each one of you is doing. I have created each of you and fashioned you individually and I know every detail of everyone of you.[56] I know every thought that passes through your mind. I know every intent of your heart.[57] I know every motive that is behind every action that you take. I know much more about you than you do about yourselves and you are fascinating creatures indeed. You are wondrously made and you keep Me occupied all the time. I delight in you. Even when you are against Me I delight in what I have created for I see you exercising the free will that I gave you. I delight in you and I love you even though I do not always delight in what you do. I am never against you but I am against your enemy Satan and I see how he deceives and manipulates you. So I am not against you. I delight in you and I long for you to turn back to Me so that I can have a relationship with you. Do not think that I do not see what you do in secret.[58] Do not think that I will not notice. You can keep nothing from Me for I am all-seeing and all-knowing. I even know what you will think before you think it, what you will do before you do it. I know every thought and every intent of your heart. So do not try to hide anything from Me for I already know. Instead be open and honest with Me and come to Me and share your lives with Me for I long for you to involve Me in your lives. You only have to repent and turn to Me and I am there for you, for I have already paid the price for all the evil that you think and do.[59] So yes, I am watching and I am considering and understanding all the works of men, and I long for you to include Me in what you think and do.

Psalm 33:16–17

AUTHOR *Lord, what do You mean in these verses?*

FATHER I am saying that you cannot rely on natural

means to deliver you from evil. I am your strong tower.[60] I am your shield and I am your deliverer.[61] Do not rely on natural means but come to Me for help against the enemy, whether it is a natural enemy or a spiritual enemy. Armies cannot save you. Great strength cannot save you. Horses cannot save you and neither can the modern equivalent of tanks, planes and ships. Look to Me as your deliverer in times of stress and in times of trial, whether your trial is on an individual level or on a national level. I can deliver individuals and I can deliver nations. My arm is not shortened that I cannot save.[62] My ability is not weakened. Whatever your trial, national or individual, turn to Me and I will deliver you. I will always deliver those who put their trust in Me and do not rely on their own strength but look to Me for deliverance. Have I not proved this over and over again down the ages? No, do not rely on natural solutions to problems but turn to Me and I will show you what to do and how to do it. The individual who prays to Me in their distress, and the nation who prays to Me in their distress, I will deliver, for I am your strength, I am your shield, I am your strong tower and I am your deliverer, says your Lord. Whatever your problem, turn to Me for help for nothing is too difficult for Me,[63] and I love you, says your God.

Psalm 33:18–19

FATHER My children, I am watching out for you. If you fear Me, if you honour and obey Me, then I am watching out for you. My eyes run to and fro throughout the whole earth to show Myself strong on behalf of those whose heart is perfect towards Me.[64] If you will put your trust in Me instead of in the strength of this world then I will deliver you, I will show you mercy and I will sustain and keep you in all circumstances. Put your trust in Me and not in the world. I am much more able to save you than the world. In fact the world cannot save you. I alone am your strong Redeemer.[65] I alone can save your soul from destruction or your body from famine. So turn to Me and I will deliver you from the snare of the fowler and the perilous pestilence.[66] I will save you from death and I will keep you alive for evermore. In Me alone is salvation for your spirit, your soul and your body. Behold I am watching for you to turn to Me, for I am ready and able and willing to deliver you and set you free.

Psalm 33:20

AUTHOR *Lord, how are You our help and shield?*

FATHER I am your very present help in time of trouble.[67] If you will turn to Me and put your trust in Me then I will be able to help you and protect you from all evil. However, you must put your trust in Me. I cannot help you if you always look to your own resources or for help from the world. If you do that then you limit My ability to help you for I cannot go beyond the limits that you draw. I have given you free will and I will respect that. I have set Myself boundaries over which I will not go and one of those boundaries is not to go against your free will. Therefore it is necessary for you to turn to Me and seek My help before I can help you. But if you will turn to Me and seek My help and trust Me to work things out for you then you will see Me at work in your lives. Cast all your care onto Me[68] and I will deliver you. I will set you free and I will be your shield and your very present help in times of trouble.

Psalm 33:21

FATHER If you will put your trust in Me then you shall rejoice in times to come. You will see Me move in miraculous ways on your behalf. You will see the enemy fall like lightning from the sky,[69] you will see opposition crumble before you, and you will see many signs and wonders. You will be amazed at what I will do and how I will work in what seems to be impossible situations. Remember that I specialise in doing the impossible. Nothing is too difficult for Me and I delight in seeing you stand in awe of what I have done. Yes, your heart will rejoice if you put your trust in My Holy name for I am your strong deliverer, I am your strong tower and I am your shield and your fortress. If I am for you then who can be against you?[70] Trust Me then with all your problems. Fret not, worry not. Put your hand in the hand of your Father who loves you and all will be well, for He will look after you and keep you and deliver you from the snare of the fowler and from the perilous pestilence. No harm shall befall you for I have given My angels charge over you to keep you in all your ways.[71]

Psalm 33:22

AUTHOR *Will Your mercy be upon us, Lord?*

FATHER Yes My mercy shall be upon you for I am a merciful God and it is My nature always to have mercy.[72] But notice that I have said that My mercy shall be upon you as you put your hope in Me. Notice that My mercy does not come automatically. There is a relationship between you putting your hope in Me and My mercy flowing to you. As I have said before, I have chosen to place boundaries on Myself that are related to your free will. Therefore, to the degree that you put your hope and your trust in Me, to that degree will you release My mercy towards you. It is you who puts limits on Me and not Me Myself. The more you put your trust in Me the more you shall release My mercy towards you. Put all your hope and all your trust in Me therefore and you shall release all My mercy towards you. It is not that I seek to withhold from you unless you twist My arm, but that I have created you to be free beings to interact with Me. I have given you a part to play in our relationship so that you can exercise your free wills. I have deliberately chosen to limit Myself in this way to give you the opportunity to play your part. There is therefore a direct correlation between you putting your trust and hope in Me and the degree to which I can release My mercy to you. Therefore My mercy shall be upon you, just as you hope in Me. Hope therefore in Me. Put your trust in Me. Involve Me in what you are doing and in the problems that you have for I want to be involved in your lives. I love you, you are My children and I want a relationship with you. It is to have this relationship with you that I have chosen to place these limits upon Myself. Our relationship is what matters to Me above everything else because I love you, My children. I love you indeed.

Psalm Thirty-four

Psalm 34:1

AUTHOR *Lord, how do we bless You at all times?*

FATHER My children, you bless Me when you kneel down in adoration with a song of praise on your lips. I want you to bless Me at all times. Now, I obviously don't want you to spend your whole lives on your knees singing hymns of praise to Me. It is not the kneeling that blesses Me and it is not the singing that blesses Me but it is what they represent, what they are a symbol of that blesses Me. When you kneel down before Me you are saying to Me that I am your Lord and that you are submitting your will to Mine. That blesses Me, for that humble submission opens the door for Me to bless you. When you are proud and arrogant, stiff necked and intent upon going your own way and doing your own thing, then you make it impossible for Me to bless you. It is the humble and contrite heart that opens the door to My blessings.[1] And I am blessed when I am able to bless you because I love you, for you are My children. You bless Me when you sing hymns of praise to Me, for in your worship and giving of thanks, again, I am able to respond to you with more blessing. So, My children, if you are to bless Me at all times then what I require of you is not that you constantly kneel before Me but that you constantly have the attitude towards Me that the kneeling symbolises. I want you to have your wills constantly submitted to Mine. I want you at all times to be humble before Me, to be soft and pliable before Me, seeking My will and not your own. If you constantly have this attitude, if you 'kneel' before Me at all times, then I will be blessed indeed for then you will open the door for Me to pour out blessing upon you. And it is in blessing you that I am blessed. Then you shall have hymns of praise on your lips as you rejoice in what I am doing in your lives.

Psalm 34:2

AUTHOR *What does it mean for my soul to make its boast in the Lord?*

FATHER As you kneel before Me and I pour out My blessing upon you, then you shall rejoice and praise Me. Your soul (your mind, will and emotions) will express what is in your spirit. Your spirit already rejoices in Me, for your spirit is born of My Spirit.[2] Your spirit is constantly praising Me and rejoicing in Me. As I bless you, your soul too will rejoice in what you see Me do. You will boast of what I am doing in your lives. You will be so full of rejoicing that you will not be able to contain it and you will have to tell others of what I have done in your lives. As you boast of Me then, others who are depressed and pushed down by their circumstances and the enemy, will rejoice too for they will see a way out of their trouble. Your rejoicing and your celebration of what I have done for you will cause others to have hope and they too will turn to Me as you explain to them the reason for your rejoicing.

Psalm 34:3

AUTHOR *How do we magnify You, Lord?*

FATHER You magnify Me by making Me look bigger in the eyes of others. To many people I am very small and insignificant, if they believe that I exist at all. If you will exalt My name by rejoicing and boasting in who I am, and in what I have done for you, then you will magnify Me in the sight of those who do not know Me. You are My witnesses. You are My representatives. The people will only know of Me in the first instance by how you portray Me to them. You are their first contact. How can they come to Me and know Me for themselves unless you first magnify My name to them so that they take notice of Me. It is as they see how big I am in your lives that they will realise that I am missing from their own. So exalt My name. Lift Me up, magnify Me in their sight as you rejoice in Me and boast of Me and declare how important I am to you. As you do this they will be attracted to Me and come to Me and know Me for themselves.

Psalm 34:4

AUTHOR *Do You hear us, Lord, when we seek you?*

FATHER Yes I hear you. Every time you cry to Me I hear you. My ears are constantly strained to listen for your cry. I desire to hear your voice more than anything. I always hear My children when they cry out to Me and I hear you the moment you speak. Your cry comes straight to Me. I know that sometimes it feels to you as though the heavens are brass and that you are not getting through to Me, but you must believe that even then I hear your cry the moment you call to Me.[3] The problem is more with you hearing Me than getting Me to hear you. I hear every cry that is uttered on the earth and the moment a person calls out to Me, whether they are My child yet or not, I hear them and I answer them. Sometimes My reply does not come in a form that you easily recognise and you will have to train your spiritual ears to hear Me,[4] but believe that I do hear you and that I do answer you. I will never ignore anyone who calls on My name, for I am a faithful God who keeps covenant and mercy.[5]

AUTHOR *And will You deliver us from all our fears?*

FATHER 'Fear not!' is an instruction that I have placed throughout My word. If you truly trust in Me then you will have no reason to fear, for I am love and I am perfect, and perfect love casts out all fear.[6] If I live in you by My Spirit then how can you fear, for Perfect Love lives in you and Perfect Love casts out fear. Fear is the opposite of faith. Fear is faith in what the enemy can do. If you have faith in Me then how can you have faith in the enemy? Keep your eyes fixed on Me and have faith in Me. Believe My word. Believe that I will do what I say.[7] Believe that My word is true and that it cannot fail, for I am true and cannot fail.[8] Believe that I love you. Believe that I am for you, and if I am for you then who can stand against you.[9] Allow Me to perfect love in you and then all fear will be cast out and you shall be delivered from fear.[10]

Psalm 34:5

AUTHOR *Why were they radiant when they looked to You?*

FATHER If you look to Me and come into My presence then you will be radiant. If you allow Me to perfect love in you then you shall shine with My presence. Anyone who spends time in My presence will be radiant. Did not the face of Moses shine when he had been in My presence?[11] Did not the face of Stephen shine when He beheld Me at his death?[12] If you look to Me and spend time in My presence then you too will radiate My presence and My glory to those around you.

AUTHOR *Why were their faces not ashamed?*

FATHER No one who puts their hope and their trust in Me will be ashamed for I will not let you down. I will never give you the opportunity to speak ill of My name. I am very protective of My name, and those who put their trust in My name will never be ashamed of having done so. I am faithful and I will deliver all who put their trust in Me.

Psalm 34:6

AUTHOR *Will You hear any poor man who cries to You?*

FATHER Yes I will. It does not matter who he is or what he has done or what mess he has got into. I will always hear and I will always answer anyone who cries out to Me for help; for it is the desire of My heart to rescue those whom Satan has deceived and enslaved. I am not angry with men for I know what the enemy has done. I poured out My anger against men on My Son Jesus[13] and now I have no anger against men – unless they continue to reject Me, having understood My Salvation and chosen to ignore Him.[14] Then I will be angry indeed.[15] But no, I am not angry against a sinner who repents. Therefore I will hear anyone who cries to Me and I will come to them and deliver them from the pit and the miry clay that their sin has entrapped them in. So if any poor man cries to Me I will hear him and deliver him from his troubles.

Psalm 34:7

AUTHOR *Lord, what does it mean for the angel of the Lord to encamp all around us?*

FATHER I have given My angels charge over you.[16] My angels are My servants and the charge I have given to certain of them is to surround you and minister to you and to ensure that you are kept safe whilst you fulfil your calling.[17] My angels are your servants and they are there to protect you. They encircle you. Although you cannot see them unless I open your eyes, they are indeed there. Remember Elisha and his servant.[18] Elisha knew by faith that the angels were there and that the host of angels sent to protect him was greater than the hosts arrayed against him but his servant did not have that faith. When his eyes were opened he was able to see the angels. It is not necessary for you to see the angels that surround you but they are there nevertheless. Only believe and call on them and they will protect you and deliver you from your enemies. Are there not many testimonies of miraculous intervention by angels when My people called on them? But you do need to call on them. They respond to My word and if you speak My word they will act. They will only intervene at your request. You must therefore call on them if you require their assistance. Did not Jesus say that He could call on twelve legions of angels,[19] but He did not call and therefore they did not assist Him. So many of you leave your angels standing idly by and do not use them. They are your servants not your masters. They will only respond to My word. So believe that you have angels encamped all around you to deliver you from your troubles and call on them. You have only to speak My word and they will step in and assist you. But if you do not call on them to act they will do nothing. Believe in your angels and call on them when you need help and they will deliver you, for that is what I have assigned them to do – to heed the voice of My word.

Psalm 34:8

AUTHOR *Lord, what does it mean for us to taste and see that You are good?*

FATHER It means to believe what I say and act on it. It means to act as though you believe what I say. It means to put Me to the test, in the sense that you step out in faith to act on My word to see if I will fulfil My word. Did I not say in relation to tithes and offerings, 'Put Me to the test and see if I will not open for you the windows of heaven'.[20] I will indeed honour My word, so believe what I say and see if you will not be blessed. Try Me and see if you will not be blessed. Put your trust in Me and you will be rewarded. O taste and see that I am good. You will not be disappointed.

Psalm 34:9

AUTHOR *What does it mean to fear You, Lord?*

FATHER To obey Me, to believe what I say and to act upon it. To respect My name and who I am. If you fear Me you will obey Me and honour Me because you love Me. You will not treat Me lightly and as of no consequence. I will be first in your life and you will honour Me in all that you do and say.

AUTHOR *And why is there no lack to those who fear You?*

FATHER You will have no lack because if you fear Me I will bless you. It is My desire to bless you and for you to have abundance. Do you not want your children to have plenty? Do you not want your children to be blessed? How much more then shall I want to bless you – My children. The reason I want you to fear Me is because I want to be able to bless you. If you will not fear Me, and do not honour and obey Me, then how can I get the blessing to you, for it is in obeying My word that the blessing comes.[21] I do not want you to fear Me for My benefit, but for yours. My desire is to abundantly bless you but I can only do this if you will fear Me, obey My word and do what I tell you to do. If you will do this then you will have no lack.

Psalm 34:10

AUTHOR *Why do the young lions lack and suffer hunger?*

FATHER It was not always so. When I first created the earth I created abundance. There were no shortages and there was nothing lacking. There was food for all. I did not create shortage and lack. This occurred after the fall of mankind. Then the curse came upon the earth.[22] Shortage and lack are part of the curse and I can only come against them to the degree that people fear Me and obey My word. This earth is still under the curse, and will be, until it is lifted when the sons of God are revealed.[23] Then there will be abundance again. But for now prosperity depends on submission to Me and My word. Where a people, as a nation, honour Me there is abundance.[24] Where a people dishonour Me there is lack.[25] Where individuals honour Me they will have abundance and where they dishonour Me they will have lack. This is not stick and carrot, reward and punishment, but cause and effect. It is outside of My control because I have set in place principles, and it is only as people honour and obey Me that I can step in and reverse the curse that you brought on the earth through your disobedience. So yes, the young lions may suffer lack, for the whole of creation is still under the curse, but if you will seek Me and fear Me then I can ensure that you will not lack any good thing.

Psalm 34:11

AUTHOR *How will You teach us to fear You?*

FATHER My Spirit is your teacher.[26] Listen to Him. He will interpret My word for you and speak into your spirit.[27] Learn to listen to His voice. Train yourself to be sensitive to Him and you will learn of Him.

Psalm 34:12

FATHER Do you desire life and to live many days?[28] If you will listen to My Spirit within you then He shall lead you into the way of life instead of the way of destruction. He is the Spirit of life.

Psalm 34:13

AUTHOR *Lord, what does it mean for us to keep our tongues from evil and our lips from speaking guile?*

FATHER Ah, My people, this is the most important lesson that you will ever learn, that of how to control your tongue. Your tongue can set a forest ablaze in a moment.[29] In your tongue you have the power to destroy and the power to build up. In your tongue you have the power of life and death.[30] In your tongue you have the power to control and direct your life, and the lives of others,[31] particularly those over whom you have any kind of relational authority. You really do need to learn how to control what you say. Let your words be without guile and free from evil speech.[32] Let your 'yes' mean yes and your 'no' mean no.[33] As My people you must speak rightly at all times. You represent Me and I speak truth at all times. Do you likewise. Honour Me by speaking truth. Let no deceit come out of your mouths. Let every word that comes forth from your mouths be wholesome as a tree of life.[34] What then is evil speaking? Evil speaking is to speak anything contrary to My word, or anything that appears to agree with My word but that comes from a wrong spirit or wrong motive.[35] You must learn to speak as I would speak on all occasions. How can you do this? The Holy Spirit will teach you. But first you must study and digest My word so that you know what I have said. How can you speak as I would speak if you do not know what I have already said? Therefore study My word. Then the Holy Spirit will do the rest if you will listen to His voice. Check with Him before opening your mouths. Check with Him to see if you are about to speak from a right spirit. Check with Him that your motives are pure and that there is no guile in your speech. Check with Him that what you are about to say will build up and not tear down. Check with Him all these things before you open your mouth, and your tongue will not speak evil nor your lips speak guile.

Psalm 34:14

AUTHOR *What does it mean to depart from evil and do good?*

FATHER What is evil? Evil is anything that is contrary to My word or contrary to the right spirit of My word. By that I mean My word being taken out of context and misused, or used with motives that are themselves contrary to My word. You need to have a right spirit renewed in you so that you can rightly discern and rightly divide the word of truth.[36] This is the job of the Holy Spirit within you to teach you to do this. So you are to depart from anything that is contrary to My word. It follows, then, as I have said before, that you must know and understand My word.[37] You are to depart from anything and everything that is not in line with My word or the spirit of My word, whether it be thought or word or deed or motive. This is not as difficult as it sounds for the Holy Spirit will lead you into truth if you will train your ears to listen to His voice saying, 'This is the way, walk ye in it'.[38] Conversely He will lead you to do what is good and righteous in My sight and to do it with pure and righteous motives. Simply just listen to Him and He will guide you at all times and in all circumstances. Because you have the Holy Spirit with you at all times you do not need the law to be your guide,[39] although you do need to know My will that is contained within My law.

AUTHOR *What about seeking peace and pursuing it?*

FATHER Seek peace at all times. What is peace? Peace is shalom. Peace is everything being well with you in every area of your lives. Peace is nothing broken and nothing missing. Peace is wholeness. Seek everything being whole in your lives, whether it is relationships, health, finances or whatever area of your life concerns you. Seek wholeness in this area. Pursue wholeness, but do it by seeking Me, for I am your peace. I am your wholeness. Therefore when you seek and pursue peace seek after Me and pursue Me and you will find peace.

Psalm 34:15

AUTHOR *Lord, what does it mean for Your eyes to be on the righteous and Your ears open to their cry?*

FATHER I am watching, and I see everything that goes on. My eyes are on those who seek to do My will and obey My word, and they delight Me. I am listening to everything that they say. They are continually before Me and always in My remembrance so that I can continually do them good and pour out blessing upon them.

Psalm 34:16

AUTHOR *What does it mean for Your face to be against those who do evil?*

FATHER I am also watching those who continually do evil, those whose desire is to disobey My word and whose desire is to do evil continually. I am not against a sinner who repents, for you have all gone far away from Me and done evil in My sight.[40] No, here I am talking about those whose heart is far from Me and who delight in doing wickedly.[41] I have no pleasure in them for they will not repent even when given the opportunity. No, there are those who delight in doing the will of My enemy Satan, and My face is turned against them. This does not mean that I will not give them the opportunity to repent. I will. I give everyone that opportunity. But these people I know will not take that opportunity and just as I hardened Pharoah's heart I will harden theirs and I will turn My face against them.[42] They shall never see My face or enter My presence. They shall be cut off from the earth forever. They shall have no fellowship with the congregation of the saints; neither shall they dwell on the earth any more. When I come to establish My kingdom they shall be cut off. Evildoers will not inherit the earth, but the meek shall inherit the earth.[43] So do not be one who hardens his heart towards Me but repent now while you can. Turn from your evil ways and come to Me and I will receive you and turn My face towards you, and you shall inherit the earth and partake of My kingdom and its blessings.

Psalm 34:17–18

FATHER O be righteous, people.[44] Seek righteousness. Seek to do what is right in My sight. Seek after Me with all that is in you and I will hear your cry and come to your aid. I am near those who have a broken and contrite heart. I am just waiting to hear you say the word and I will be there for you. You do not need to be cut off from the earth. You do not need to have My face turned from you. All you have to do is repent and call on My name and I will save you,[45] for it is My desire that all shall be saved and that none should perish.[46]

Psalm 34:19

AUTHOR *What are the afflictions of the righteous? Why should we have afflictions if we are righteous and seek to do Your will?*

FATHER Was not My Son Jesus righteous and did He not seek to do My will and was not He afflicted?[47] Many were His afflictions and His sorrows but I delivered Him out of them. Do not think that you will not have afflictions because you are righteous. Was not Paul righteous and did not he seek to do My will, yet many were his afflictions.[48] My children, I am not calling you to a bed of roses; yet I am, for in a bed of roses are beautiful flowers and wonderful scent and yet there are thorns. My children, in your walk with Me you will have beautiful flowers and heavenly scent but you will also have the thorns. The flowers and the scent come from Me but the thorns, the pricks, come from the enemy.[49] I will pour out blessing upon you but persecutions will come from those who delight in evil.[50] So be prepared, My people, you will have afflictions, particularly as this age draws to its close and the gross darkness covers the earth.[51] As your glory increases so will your afflictions. This is the nature of things in this age, so be prepared but fear not. I say again, 'Fear not'! for I will deliver you out of all your afflictions, as I delivered Paul and as I delivered My Son, Jesus.

Psalm 34:20

AUTHOR *Why will the bones of the righteous not be broken?*

FATHER This was a prophetic word concerning My Son Jesus in fulfilment of the law of the old covenant.[52] But I will guard you, too. I will protect you and I will deliver you.

Psalm 34:21

AUTHOR *Lord, what do You mean by evil slaying the wicked?*

FATHER A man shall reap what he sows.[53] If a man will sow into wickedness and evil then he shall ultimately reap the reward of wickedness and the reward of evil. The wages of sin is death[54] and death is separation from Me forever. Do not be deceived, there is a day of judgement to come, there is a day of reckoning to come, and a man will have to account for his wickedness.[55] You can only escape the consequences of your sin if you repent and seek after Me.[56] You can only escape the consequences of your sin by laying that sin on My Son Jesus and accepting in exchange His robe of righteousness, for then you will be able to come directly into My presence.[57] But make no mistake, be under no illusion, the man who loves evil and hates righteousness will reap a harvest from what he has sown, and that harvest of death will slay him, and he will be condemned to an eternity outside of My presence along with his lord and master, Satan.[58]

Psalm 34:22

FATHER However, I will redeem the soul of those who repent and turn to Me for salvation. My Son has paid the price for your sin. My Son has bought you back from slavery to your enemy Satan. My Son has redeemed you and set you free.[59] He has clothed you in His righteousness and brought you into My presence again.[60] If you appropriate what He has done for you and call on His name and make Him your Lord, then you shall never be ashamed and neither will you be judged or condemned, for I judged and condemned Him in your place. Put your trust in Him and you shall spend eternity with Me in My kingdom as My beloved child and heir, and you shall be blessed indeed.

Psalm Thirty-seven

Psalm 37:1

AUTHOR *Lord, why should we not fret because of evil doers and be envious of workers of iniquity?*

FATHER Why should you get worked up and upset because of evildoers? Their times are in My hands, just as are yours.[1] Why should you be envious of workers of iniquity for what do they have compared to you? I know that it sometimes seems as though those who are My enemies prosper, but remember that the sun shines on both the just and the unjust.[2] The same laws that I have set in place for you will work for them too – for a season. But remember that you will all reap what you sow and that workers of iniquity will in due season reap the rewards of their iniquity.[3] Though they seem to prosper for a season, though they seem to be blessed for a season in all that they do, it is only for a season unless they repent and turn back to Me. So why should you be envious of them if things seem to go well with them for a season? In the end what will they have? In the end what will they inherit? You, My people, the sons of the kingdom, will inherit the kingdom and they, the sons of the darkness, will inherit the darkness.[4] Keep your eyes fixed on the long term and not the short term. Keep your eyes on Me. If the wicked seem to prosper, then rejoice for them and pray for them that they will turn to Me[5] and that they will bring that prosperity into the kingdom. Do not fret, do not be envious, for these emotions are destructive. They will destroy you and stop you coming into your blessing. You keep your eyes on Me and rejoice in Me, and know that the times and the seasons for all men are in My hands and that I am a God of equity and that I will see that righteousness prevails. But remember that it is in My heart to bless and to prosper all men, even the wicked and the evil doers if they will turn back to Me. That is My heart; that the evil doers and the workers of iniquity will repent and come to Me. And remember also My people that you too were once such as they. Did you not work iniquity? Were you not an evildoer and have I not prospered you? It is only by grace that you have been saved,[6] and it is by grace that they too shall be saved.

Psalm 37:2

AUTHOR *Why will they be cut down like grass?*

FATHER It may seem to you as though evil doers are prospering in their wickedness, but it shall only be for a short season. You must remember that what seems like a lifetime to you is only a moment to Me, a moment in eternity. Just as the grass is cut down and withers in your lifetime so shall the prosperity of the wicked be in eternity. They shall reap the harvest from what they have sown and their prosperity shall be gone as though it never was – unless they turn to Me and repent.

Psalm 37:3

AUTHOR *Lord, what does it mean to trust in You?*

FATHER Have confidence in Me. In all that you do trust Me. Trust My word that it shall not fail you. Do not look at the workers of iniquity to see what they are doing and how they are fairing but keep your eyes fixed on Me, the author and finisher of your faith.[7] Keep your eyes on Me, and do what you see Me do, obey My word and trust that I will bless you and provide your needs.[8] You will see the wicked prosper for a season out of their wickedness and you will wonder, 'Why am I not prospering like they are? Here I am obeying the word and all I seem to get is trouble'. No, do not look at them, for their prosperity is for a season only and they shall be cut down like the grass. Do not look at them, do not be envious of them, for they shall not inherit the earth. No My children, keep your eyes fixed on Me and put your trust in Me alone and you shall see that I will indeed prosper you.

AUTHOR *What does it mean to do good?*

FATHER Obey My word, do what I would do, say what I would say. Be like Me. Be like Jesus. Listen to the Holy Spirit and He shall lead you to do what is good and right in My sight.

AUTHOR *What does it mean to dwell in the land and feed on Your faithfulness?*

FATHER I am a faithful God who keeps covenant and mercy.[9] What I have said I will do, that I will do. I have placed you in the world and in the land and you must dwell in the land that I have given you. Dwell amongst those whom I have placed you amongst and be My ambassadors.[10] I have placed you there to tell others of Me. There is no other reason for you to dwell in this land, for you could come and dwell with Me if I did not have work for you to do. No, dwell in the land, do good and feed on My faithfulness. Because I have called you I will supply all your needs. Have I not said that I already know what you need before you ask?[11] So just ask Me and I will give to you all you need to fulfil the work that I have called you to do in the land that I have called you to dwell in.[12] Do not look to the world to supply your needs but look to Me. Now that does not mean that you can sit back and do nothing and not work,[13] but it does mean that your trust should be in Me and not in the world system in which you dwell. Feed on My faithfulness for the world system cannot be trusted as you well know.

Psalm 37:4

AUTHOR *Lord, what does it mean for us to delight ourselves in You?*

FATHER It means for you to have pleasure in flowing together with Me and what I am doing. It means for you to be soft and pliable so that I can mould you into what I want you to be. You see, I have desires for you. I have a goal and a target for what I want you to become. I have plans and purposes for your life that are beyond anything that you could imagine for yourself,[14] and it is a delight to Me when you flow with Me, when you are soft and pliable in My hands, for then I can fulfil My plan for you. I am the potter and you are the clay.[15] When the clay is soft and pliable in the hands of the potter then he can mould that clay into a beautiful object. What begins as a lump of earth becomes a beautiful vessel in his hand. Are you not lumps of earth?[16] Are you not adam – red earth, and am I not the potter? I have beautiful objects in mind that I want to create out of you.[17] But if the clay is lumpy, stiff, dry and brittle how can the potter mould it? He cannot, for it will break apart in his hands. The clay must be moist, soft and pliable for it to be a delight to the potter to use. You are clay in My hands and if you are soft and pliable beneath My fingers then I can do with you wondrous things, things you would never dream of. Allow the Holy Spirit to make you soft and pliable. Soak yourself in Him and He will make you a delight to Me.

AUTHOR *Lord, what about giving us the desires of our heart?*

FATHER If you delight yourself in Me and allow Me to mould you into what I want you to be then I can place in you the desires that I have for you. I can make My desires for you to be your desires too. If we both desire the same thing then I can see to it that you fulfil those desires. Do not resist Me, My people. Do not be stiff and unyielding under My hands for I have only good plans for you, only good desires for you.[18] Make yourselves soft and pliable, bend your will to Mine, and I will place in you desires that are beyond your wildest dreams. I will give you the desires of your heart and when I have given you the desire I will see to it that that desire in you is fulfilled. I will not give you a desire and then not fulfil it. So, My people, as long as you are soft and pliable under My hands, as long as you delight yourself in Me, as long as you allow the Holy Spirit to lead and direct you, follow the desires of your heart and seek to see them fulfilled, for I have given you those desires. They are of Me, says your Lord.

Psalm 37:5

AUTHOR *Lord, what does it mean for us to commit our way to You?*

FATHER As I have said, I will give you desires in your heart if you are soft and pliable in My hands. Trust that those desires are Godly desires given to you by Me, provided of course that those desires that you have are not contrary to My word, for I will not give you such desires as those. They clearly will have come either from the enemy or from your own evil intent.[19] No, I am not talking about those desires, but the desires that come into your heart from Me. Trust those desires and follow them. Believe that they are from Me and seek to fulfil them by committing them to Me. Roll your way over onto Me and let Me bring them to pass. If the desire is from Me then I will see to it that it will happen, if you put your trust in Me and allow Me to work My way in your life. I am talking about following the leads that I give you, following the promptings of My Holy Spirit and following the desire of your heart. If it is from Me you will not have to force things to happen. Put your trust in Me and allow Me to organise the times and the seasons.[20] Wait for My timing. Wait for the openings I give you and do not worry. Roll the care of it onto Me and watch Me bring your desire to fulfilment.[21]

Psalm 37:6

AUTHOR *What does it mean for our righteousness to be brought forth as the light and our justice as the noonday?*

FATHER If you will commit your way to Me and follow the desires that I give you, I shall increase righteousness and justice in you. Some of the desires in your heart will include pleasing Me and becoming more like Me, and I will surely bring those desires to pass. As long as you give Me permission I shall work in your life to increase justice and to increase righteousness. Indeed I shall work in your life to make you more like Me, and as I do that, your righteousness will shine forth and your justice shall increase and you will be as a sun shining in the gross darkness that is about to cover the earth.[22]

Psalm 37:7

AUTHOR *Lord, what does it mean to rest in You?*

FATHER Activity, activity! Why do you always want to be doing? Why can you not just be, as I AM?[23] Yes, there are things for you to do and I have plans for you to fulfil, but let them be fulfilled in My time. I am not in a rush. I am not pressured, for I have eternity in which to accomplish My desires. Learn of Me and come to Me all you who are burdened and heavy laden and I will give you rest.[24] Learn to relax, learn to rest. Learn to rest in Me and conform to My timetable. If you will listen to My Spirit within you, if you will listen to His voice, then He will direct you. He will direct you to take up work and He will direct you to put down work. He will direct you to take up activity and He will direct you to put down activity. He will direct you to labour and He will direct you to rest. What I am saying is that there is a time for everything under heaven.[25] There is a time to be busy and there is a time to rest. Do not neglect the one for the other. There is no merit in wearing yourselves out on My behalf. I do not require that of you and it does not please Me. What pleases Me is that you spend time in My presence listening to My voice, so that I can direct you into fruitful activity.[26] Not all activity is fruitful. Not all activity is from Me. Learn to rest. Learn to listen to the voice of the Spirit so that He can direct you into fruitful activity.

AUTHOR *And what about waiting patiently for You?*

FATHER Do not run ahead of Me. Do not try to rush Me or pressure Me. I have a perfect plan. I am working out the times and the seasons. I am manipulating people and events so that My plans come together. I love it when a plan comes together. So, do not rush Me. Wait patiently for Me, even if it seems as though nothing is happening and nothing is working. Know that I am at work behind the scenes and if you will wait patiently for Me you will see a 'suddenly'. Suddenly things will fall into place. Suddenly it will happen. Suddenly there will be a way when it seemed as though there was no way, and it will be effortless. If you will wait patiently for Me there will be no pressure, you will not have to force things and then the Spirit will say to you, 'Do this and do that', and suddenly what you have been striving to produce on your own will fall into place and happen. So do not strive, do not fret; listen to Me, wait patiently for Me, and then move when I tell you to move and suddenly you will see the fruit of your labour and there will be no sorrow with it.

AUTHOR *What about the man who brings wicked schemes to pass?*

FATHER Do not fret because of him. As I have already told you, his times and his seasons are in My hands also. Leave such a man to Me and I will deal with him.[27] You pray for such a man, that he will open his ears to hear My voice so that I can direct his paths also. But do not be concerned about his activities. Do not come against him. Pray for him, not against him, and leave him to Me, and you will be amazed at what I will do.

Psalm 37:8

AUTHOR *Lord, should we cease from all anger and forsake all wrath?*

FATHER No My son, not all anger and all wrath. There is a place for righteous anger. Did not Jesus get angry and was He not wrathful?[28] But remember at whom to direct your anger for our warfare is not against flesh and blood but against Satan.[29] Let him be the subject of your wrath. Get angry at him for what he is doing in the lives of people and for what he is doing in the world. Remember that the wicked man and the foolish man is being manipulated by the enemy, and this is why I have told you to pray for that man and not to vent your anger on him. Pray for his eyes and ears to be opened so that he might understand, for if he understood surely he would forsake his wicked ways, just as you did, and turn to Me. Yes there is a place for anger and a place for wrath but direct that anger and wrath at the enemy and come against him with the authority that I have given you.

AUTHOR *Are You saying then that we should not be angry with people at all?*

FATHER Not entirely. Anger is an emotion that I have given you. Anger is a natural emotion to have when people treat you wrongly, when they are unjust towards you or when they hurt you and those you love. It is natural that you will feel anger in these circumstances. It is not the anger that is wrong; it is what you do with that anger that is important.[30] I have told you not to fret for a reason. Fretting or worry, or meditating on your anger or on the wrong that has been done you will only cause destruction. It will cause destruction to the object of your anger and it will cause destruction to you. When you meditate in anger on a wrong that has been done to you then you magnify that wrong and it gets greater and greater in your eyes until it becomes an insurmountable mountain. It becomes as a great tree with a root of bitterness that goes deep into the ground of your soul, and a root of bitterness will poison the whole tree that grows from it.[31] A root of bitterness will poison your whole life and cause you to move far from Me. This is why I tell you not to fret over evildoers, because I know that fretting will cause this root of bitterness to grow in your life and I know how destructive that can be. It will cause you to seek ways of getting revenge on the person who has wronged you. It will cause you to plot to do evil, and you may cause destruction to the person who has wronged you and you may get your revenge, but you will destroy your own soul in the process.[32] Do not fret over evil doers and over those who have hurt and wronged you. Be angry, that is a natural emotion to feel, but do not allow the sun to go down on your wrath.[33]

I have given you instruction as to what to do with your anger. First of all know that the wrongdoer is being used and manipulated by Satan. Therefore direct your anger at him and not at the person who has hurt you.[34] Pray for the person who has hurt you.[35] Forgive the person who has hurt you. This is a commandment. You must do this, and I will give you the grace to do this, if you will be willing to obey Me. You must forgive the person who has wronged you so that I can forgive you your sin.[36] You are not perfect. You have wronged others and you need forgiveness too. If you insist on implementing the law for others then I must bring the force of the law to bear on you, and the wages of sin is death.[37] Therefore you must forgive others so that I can forgive you. You must extend grace to others so that I can extend grace to you. If you insist on retribution for others, if you insist on justice for others, then I can only extend retribution and justice to you for what you have done. Therefore for your own sake be merciful to those who have wronged you and I will be merciful to you. So do not ask for justice, do not seek revenge, but forgive those who have wronged you and I will forgive you.

There is another reason for you to forgive. You see, when you forgive then you release the anger. Anger is alright, but if you misdirect that anger and you fret over the evil done to you then that root of bitterness will grow in your life and destroy you, but if you will forgive, then the enemy is not able to cause that root to grow in you, for when you forgive then you release the anger. The enemy causes others to hurt you because he wants to establish that root of bitterness in your life that he knows will destroy you and lead you far from Me. Do not let him. Do not fall for his deceits. Forgive, and release yourself from that trap of offence that he has laid for you.[38] Instead, do not allow the sun to go down on your wrath but deal with it.[39] If possible go to the person who has wronged you and forgive them and make things right between you.[40] If you cannot do this then roll the burden of your care onto Me[41] and let Me deal with it. Have I not said that vengeance is Mine and I will repay?[42] If the evildoer will not repent, if he will not turn from his wicked ways, then leave the care of that with Me. You look to yourself[43] and do not allow Satan to entrap you with an opportunity to be offended or angry with another.[44] Instead turn your anger against him and pray diligently for the person who has offended you.[45] Vent your anger on your enemy by praying for the release of the person whom he has in his grasp. Be merciful to the one who has wronged you and I will be merciful to you. Forgive, and I will forgive you.[46] Cast your care onto Me and let Me be the one who repays, for then you will not bring justice onto your own head. So cease from anger and misplaced wrath for it will indeed only cause harm, and you will be the one who is harmed. Instead, do what I have told you to do and fix your eyes on Me and let Me deal with the person who has wronged you. You worship Me. You praise Me in all circumstances and I will fill your heart with joy. Do not give a wrong place to anger that will destroy you but instead give place to joy that will give you life forever more.

Psalm 37:9

AUTHOR *When shall the evil doers be cut off?*

FATHER There is a time for every purpose under heaven[47] and there will be a time for the wicked to be destroyed. I am a God of justice as well as a God of mercy. I will do everything in My power to persuade the evil doer to repent and turn back to Me, but I can only persuade because I have chosen to give you free will and I will allow you to exercise that free will even if it means that you will choose destruction. But make no mistake, there will be a day of judgement and there will be a day of reckoning.[48] It must come. I cannot delay forever.[49] The day will come when an account must be made, and for those who have chosen wickedness above My mercy that will indeed be a terrible day, for they will be cut off from Me forever. They will be cut off from this earth, from their fellow man and from My kingdom and they will be cast into the darkness, into the lake of fire where their worm dieth not.[50] What can I do if they choose this? What more can I do? I sent My Son to pay the price for their wickedness but they have thrown His death back in My face and blasphemed His name and they will not repent. I have no choice, even though it distresses Me greatly. I have no choice for I have given them the choice, and they have chosen. So yes the wicked will one day be cut off and there is nothing more I can do to prevent it.

AUTHOR *What do You mean by the expression, 'their worm does not die'?*

FATHER Their destruction is never ending. On earth you are used to things having a beginning and an end. Even bad things come to an end eventually. But you must understand that I am eternal, and I created you to be eternal like Me. You do not come to an end when you die; you live forever. Now, you can live in perpetual life with Me or you can live in perpetual death without Me. The wicked will live in perpetual death. They will never cease to exist. It will be as though the worm that eats their flesh will do so forever. There will be no end to it. The fire that burns their bodies will do so forever. There is no end to it. They will be in a perpetual state of torment and dying and there will be no release, no end to it, and there is nothing that I can do about it once they have finally chosen that path. It distresses Me to even talk about it for they have no concept of what they are choosing. I cannot get them to understand. If they did understand they would not choose death over life. So many of you choose death over life thinking that death will be an end to your problems, that death will bring peace and a state of non-existence. But it does not! There is no end, for you are eternal. You will always be, either in perpetual life or in perpetual dying, but there will be no end. There is no peace in death. There is only peace in life, and there is only life in Me.[51] O choose life, My people, choose life.[52] Do not choose death for you do not understand what it is that you are choosing. Why will you not repent? Why will you not accept the salvation that I have bought for you through the death of My Son? Listen; today I have set before you a choice. It is your choice; you choose. You either choose Me and choose life, or you choose Satan and choose death. It is one or the other. There is no halfway, no compromise. It is either life or death, blessing or cursing. You choose today whom you will serve,[53] but I say to you one more time – choose life!

AUTHOR *Lord, what does it mean for us to wait on You?*

JESUS It means for you to be patient and wait for your reward. I have given you a hope, I have given you a future, and I have given you a purpose under heaven.[54] Just as there will be a day when the wicked shall be cut off, there will be a day when the meek shall inherit the earth. Those who choose Me as their Lord choose life, and those who choose life will live forever on the earth in My kingdom. They shall have blessing forever more, and they shall have fellowship with Me forever more, and they shall live in glorious light forever more, and they shall be at peace. All you have to do to choose life is to turn away from your sin and call on Me. Call My name and ask Me to be your Lord. Ask Me to save you and I will.[55] It is My desire that you should be saved.[56] I died that you might be saved. Call on My name and I will give you a place in My Father's kingdom.

AUTHOR *But what does it mean for us to wait on You?*

FATHER Wait patiently for what you will inherit. To wait on Me means to serve Me, to attend to Me, to obey My word and to do what I ask you to do. It means to do this in the confident expectation that you will reap your reward,[57] that you will inherit the earth at the appointed time. It means to expect My word to be fulfilled in every aspect and that you will one day come into what I have promised you.

Psalm 37:10

AUTHOR *Lord, what is a little while?*

JESUS There is an appointed time for the consummation of things.[58] I have given you signposts in My word when that shall be, and it shall be soon. In the meantime the wicked shall increase and do wickedly and the righteous shall increase in their righteousness. So until the appointed time the wicked will continue, but then they shall be cut off. The appointed time is coming closer and it will be only a little while. Watch the signs, for I am coming soon.

AUTHOR *Why will we look diligently for the place of the wicked and it shall be no more?*

JESUS When I come I shall establish My rule with a rod of iron[59] and I will utterly remove the wicked from the earth. I shall establish My kingdom in righteousness and there will be no place for the workers of iniquity in that kingdom. There is a place set aside for them and they will be banished there.

Psalm 37:11

AUTHOR *What does it mean for the meek to inherit the earth, and who are the meek?*

FATHER The meek are those who will be obedient to My word. The proud and haughty man is a man who thinks he knows better than Me; he is a man who ignores Me, ignores My word and does only that which seems right in his own eyes. He is a man who denies My existence, or chooses to ignore Me even if he does believe I exist. Such a man as this will not inherit the earth, neither shall he have any place in My kingdom, nor any part of Me. The meek man is the man who recognises I exist and who humbles himself before Me and seeks to obey My word at every opportunity. Such a man as this I can use and he will have a part in Me and My kingdom, and he will inherit the earth.[60]

AUTHOR *What does it mean to inherit the earth?*

FATHER It means to continue to live on the earth under the rulership of My Son after He has come. It means to continue to live on earth after I have reformed it and refashioned it,[61] forever. It means to be an heir to all the blessings and delights that I have established for mankind. It means to be in My presence forever, for I intend to dwell with mankind on the new earth.[62]

AUTHOR *Lord, what does it mean to delight ourselves in the abundance of peace?*

FATHER Peace means wholeness: nothing broken, nothing missing and everything being well with you. It means having more than enough of everything that you could possibly need. In My kingdom there will be no lack, there will be no sickness, no disease, and you will have everything that you need. You will delight yourselves in this abundance and you will be blessed. The curse and all its effects shall be removed from the earth[63] and you will delight in Me and My provision for you, as I originally intended that you should.

Psalm 37:12

AUTHOR *Why do the wicked plot against the just and gnash at them with their teeth?*

FATHER Light always dispels the darkness. The wicked hate the just, for their wicked deeds are brought into the light by the righteous deeds of the just. The wicked love the darkness, for the darkness hides their wickedness. When the light comes they are shown up for what they are, and therefore they hate the righteous who are the light, and they will try to destroy the bearers of that light so that they can continue in their darkness. The unrighteous and the wicked will always persecute the righteous.

Psalm 37:13

AUTHOR *Why do You laugh at them?*

FATHER I laugh at them for they cannot escape the dawn. The dawn is surely coming when the unrighteous will no longer be able to hide in the darkness. His deeds will be exposed and judgement shall come. Behold the Day Star is rising,[64] the Day Spring from on high,[65] and My Sun is rising in the east.[66] The night will soon be over and the Dawn is almost come.

Psalm 37:14–15

AUTHOR *Why will the sword of the wicked enter their own heart and their bow be broken?*

FATHER A man brings judgement on himself. As he has sown, so shall he reap.[67] He who lives by the sword shall die by the sword.[68] When the Dawn comes He will expose all that is hidden in darkness and the wicked will receive the just rewards for their deeds,[69] for they have not turned to Me in repentance and neither have they sought My forgiveness. Therefore justice must prevail instead of mercy.

Psalm 37:16–17

AUTHOR *Why is the little that a righteous man has better than the riches of the wicked?*

FATHER What the righteous man has cannot be measured in terms of money. The righteous man has Me, he has My Spirit, and he has My Word. What more could a man want, for he has My wisdom; and My wisdom will bring him the ability to get wealth,[70] and the wealth that I shall give him will have no sorrow with it.[71] The wealth that the wicked accumulates has much sorrow with it for he shall reap the rewards of what he has sown in order to get that wealth. Wealth that has been obtained through unrighteous means carries with it the reward of death. It has been gained in corruption and it will produce corruption. The righteous man will not lose the little he has, and indeed, as he deals righteously with that little, I will multiply it until he has much.[72] The unrighteous will have to fight to keep what he has gained for there will always be those who will try to take it from him. There will be much sorrow attached to wealth that has been gained through unrighteous means. And in the end the reward of unrighteousness is death, and I will take that wealth and I will give it to the righteous man to be his forever as he lives in My kingdom.

Psalm 37:18

AUTHOR *Lord, what does it mean for You to know the days of the upright?*

FATHER I know all your days, from beginning to end, from the day that I formed you in the womb until the day that you die. I have all knowledge and I know everything that you will do, everything that you will say and every thought that you will think. I know you far better than you know yourself. I know everything about you, all your coming in and all your going out. I have numbered your days and I have planned for them. However this does not mean that I have pre-ordained your days. You have free will and you make choices, and those choices are yours. You are still responsible for the choices you make. It just means that I know beforehand what you will choose to do. This is quite difficult for some of you to grasp, and you think that if I know beforehand what you will do that I have pre-ordained it and that you have no choice. This is not so. Just because I have knowledge of what choices you will make does not mean that I am directing that choice. I plan accordingly but I do not cause you to do what you do. That is up to you, and I will not remove from you the freedom to choose. Believe Me, you are free to choose, and the direction you take in your life is your responsibility. So yes, I know all your days, even before you live them, for I am outside of time and I know the end from the beginning. My perspective is totally different to yours and you cannot understand how this works at this time. But believe Me that I know your days, and I will fulfil My plans and purposes for your life without diminishing your ability to choose what path you take or absolving you from responsibility for the choices you make. And I have planned for the righteous that their inheritance will be secure in Me. Therefore make righteous decisions and take a righteous path and I will lead you into your inheritance.

Psalm 37:19

AUTHOR *Lord, why will the upright not be ashamed in the evil time?*

FATHER There is an evil time coming upon the earth when the spirit of antichrist shall arise and the wicked shall do wickedly. During this time My people, those who are called by My name, shall not be ashamed. Am I not with them? Am I not on their side? Do I not hold their goings-out and their comings-in in My hands?[73] Am I not their God and am I not their Father? My protection is upon them and My hand is with them. Therefore they shall be vindicated in the congregation and they shall be upheld by My name and they shall not be ashamed; neither shall they see corruption. I will not fail them and I shall raise them up on the last day and they shall be presented faultless before all those who have persecuted them.[74]

AUTHOR *How will they be satisfied in the days of famine, and what are the days of famine?*

FATHER There will be great lack in the earth as My hand is withdrawn because of the evil deeds of the nations,[75] but My people shall not go hungry. My people shall not be in need for I shall supply all their need according to My riches in glory.[76] As they meet the needs of others now, so shall I meet their need in the time of great famine.

Psalm 37:20

AUTHOR *And what of the wicked, Lord?*

JESUS All those who stand against Me shall perish, for I am coming to judge the earth and I will repay to each one as he has sown. I will utterly remove from the earth those who have stood against Me and there shall be no trace of them in My kingdom. Only the righteous and the just shall inherit the kingdom that has been prepared for them since the foundation of the earth.

Psalm 37:21

AUTHOR *Lord, talk to me about verse 21*

FATHER This verse shows the difference between the world's principles and kingdom principles. The world seeks to get, whereas the kingdom seeks to give. The whole ethos of the world is to get as much as possible for oneself. Self is number one. This is because the world system has been orchestrated and developed by

Satan who seeks to advance himself above everything and everyone, even Me. And those who are subject to his rule will follow his example. My principles are different. I seek to give and to bless as much as I can, and those who have subjected themselves to My rule will do the same, for they know that because I seek to give, they shall receive. Be like Me, My children, be merciful and seek opportunity to give, and as you give to others you create opportunity for Me to give to you. But if you seek to withhold and acquire for yourself, then you create opportunity for Satan to take from you what you already have, for he is a thief who comes to kill, steal and destroy, whereas I have come to give life and give it abundantly.[77] So My people seek to give rather than to receive. However, there is a time for you to receive graciously, for in receiving you give others the opportunity to give to you. Do not refuse to receive, for then you steal from others the opportunity to give. You can always give again what you have received. And in the giving I can cause abundance to flow, for I can multiply what is given and bless the whole earth with it.

Psalm 37:22

AUTHOR *What does it mean to be blessed and to be cursed?*

FATHER To be blessed is to be in My favour. To be blessed is to be in My presence. Those who seek to be in My presence and in My favour will be blessed with all that I can give them. To be blessed is to inherit the kingdom that I have prepared for you. To be blessed is to delight in Me and to have Me delight in you. To be blessed is to be My beloved child whom I dearly love. On the other hand, to be cursed is to be outside of My favour and outside of My presence so that I cannot pour out My love and affection upon you. Read Deuteronomy chapter 28. To be cursed is to be outside My umbrella of love and protection and under the control and domination of My enemy, Satan.

Psalm 37:23

AUTHOR *What does it mean for You to order the steps of a good man?*

FATHER The man who delights in Me and submits himself to Me will be open to the direction that I will give him. When you acknowledge Me in all your ways I can order your steps. I can tell you what to do and when to do it. I can tell you where to go and when to go. I can map out My plan for your life and know that I can lead you into fulfilling it. I have a plan and a purpose for your life which only you can fulfil and it gives Me great delight when you submit your way to Me and I can direct your steps and see you walk through this life on the path that I have chosen for you. It is not that I want to dictate your every move and leave you with no freedom of choice. No, I want you to choose and I want you to make your own decisions, but I delight when you choose to include Me in your decision making for then I can give you help and direction, then I can enable you to fulfil the potential that I have placed within you. It is a delight to Me when you choose to work with Me and not against Me. It is a delight to Me when we can work together as Father and son towards a common goal, for then we have fellowship together and I can enjoy your company and your companionship. Then I can take great delight in what you are able to accomplish in My name as I order your steps and we walk together in the direction you should go.

Psalm 37:24

AUTHOR *Lord, in what way do we fall and You uphold us?*

FATHER My son, as a small child you began to learn to walk. At first you clung to the furniture and pulled yourself up onto your feet. Then you tried a few steps and you fell down. So you pulled yourself up again and tried again. Eventually you were able to take those steps without falling. Soon you were able to put your hand in the hand of your father and walk with him, but as you toddled along you occasionally fell down, but because your father had hold of your hand you were not utterly cast down for he was able to pull you back up again and you continued walking beside him. This is the picture I want you to have of your walk with Me through this life. I want you to walk beside Me so that I can lead and direct you and I want you to hold My hand so that I can pull you up when you fall. You will fall, and I will let you fall, because it is in falling that you learn to walk. But I will not let you be utterly cast down, nor will I let you hurt yourself, for I love you and I want to see you succeed. As long as you keep your hand in My hand I can hold you and pull you back onto your feet.

AUTHOR *How do we keep our hand in Your hand?*

FATHER You walk close beside Me and keep in constant touch with Me. The little child walks close to her daddy and does not leave his side. She reaches up and takes hold of his hand and does not let go. My children, this is what I want you to do. I want you to keep in close and constant touch with Me by reading and studying My word, by talking to Me in prayer, by being quiet and listening to what My Spirit says to you. Consult Me in everything and expect Me to answer. If you make a mistake do not worry. If you get it wrong it will not be a disaster, for I can redeem every situation, provided you keep listening to Me and keep having fellowship with Me. To walk with your hand in My hand is to be in constant contact and to have close fellowship with Me. It is for us to walk together on the same path, side by side, sharing in all that you do and say. To walk with your hand in My hand is to put your trust in Me in every area of your life and to share your life with Me. This is what I desire as a loving parent. I do not desire to suffocate you but to share in what you do, and allow you the freedom to do it safely. As you walk with Me you shall not fear for I am by your side to keep you from harm and I have hold of your hand.

Psalm 37:25

AUTHOR *Lord, is it right that the righteous are not forsaken and never have to beg bread? It doesn't always seem like that.*

FATHER No, My son, I will never forsake the righteous, and by the righteous I mean those who are in a covenant relationship with Me. That is important – you must have entered into covenant with Me by submitting your life to Jesus and asking Him to be your Lord, then your righteousness will be of Me. It is because you are in covenant with Me that I will never forsake you or leave you. I have obligated Myself to keep the covenant that I have established through My Son Jesus, and the moment you make Him your Lord you enter into that covenant and I will make available to you all that I am and all that I have. Once you are in covenant with Me you will never lack, for I do not lack. You will never be forsaken, for in covenant you and I are one.

AUTHOR *Lord, what do You mean by us being in covenant with You?*

FATHER I am a God of covenant. You will see that from the very beginning I have entered into covenants with men, and I do not change. A covenant is a solemn agreement between two parties which is sealed by the shedding of blood. Everything that one party has belongs to the other equally. Any problems that one party has are equally the responsibility of the other. A covenant sealed in blood is unbreakable. You entered into covenant with Me. Everything you have belongs to Me, and therefore your sin became Mine. Everything I have became yours, and therefore you received My righteousness.[78] As you submit yourself to Me I become responsible for looking after you and everything I have, and all that I am, is yours, for you have given all that you have, yourself, to Me. This covenant was sealed by the blood of Jesus[79] and cannot be broken. Therefore, because your righteousness is of Me you shall never be forsaken, neither shall you beg for bread.

Psalm 37:26

AUTHOR *What does it mean for the righteous man to lend and be ever merciful?*

FATHER The righteous man will act as I would act, and My heart is to look for opportunities to bless. My nature is always to have mercy.[80] Therefore the righteous man will look for opportunities to help out his fellow man and to bless his fellow man. He will not withhold more than is right and he will sow liberally so that there will be enough for all.[81] When you give to the poor man then you lend to Me, and I will repay you.[82] As you are merciful to the poor man you show him Me, and cause him to give thanks to Me as he sees Me expressed through you.[83] And as you seek to bless others I will make sure that you and your descendants are blessed. It is the law of sowing and reaping. I have instituted this law as a fundamental part of the creation.[84] and it will work for you either for good or for evil. What you sow you will reap.[85] Therefore sow righteousness, sow liberality, sow blessing and you will reap righteousness, you will reap liberality and you will reap blessing. That is the way it works, for I have ordained it to be so.

Psalm 37:27

AUTHOR *Lord, what is the relationship between departing from evil, doing good and dwelling for evermore?*

FATHER Again, it is the law of sowing and reaping. If you sow evil you will reap evil and if you sow goodness you will reap goodness. Reaping goodness will cause you to live long in the land but reaping evil will cause you to be cut off. Therefore do good and live forevermore.

Psalm 37:28–29

FATHER I love justice and I love righteousness and I will uphold and preserve those who practise them. I will fight on behalf of the man who upholds My ways and I will fight against the man who continues to uphold the ways of My enemy Satan. As Satan was cut off from heaven[86] so will his followers be cut off from the earth. Only the righteous shall inherit the earth and be part of My kingdom.

Psalm 37:30

AUTHOR *Lord, what does it mean for the mouth of the righteous to speak wisdom and his tongue to talk of justice?*

FATHER The righteous man will renew his mind by studying and meditating My word.[87] He will not be conformed to the ways of this world and neither will he think or speak as do the people of this world. He will be like Joshua who meditated My word day and night and did not allow it to depart from his eyes. My servant Joshua was a righteous man who renewed his mind with My word. He learned to think and to speak as I think and speak and everything that he spoke was in line with My word. Because he did this he had good success in all that he did.[88] The mouth of the righteous, then, will speak My word at all times. As he meditates My word he will mutter it to himself, he will ponder it and chew it over in his mind. Because he spends much time in My word, when he speaks it will be My word that comes forth from his mouth.[89] Whenever he talks he will speak My word and he will pronounce wisdom and righteousness to those who hear him.

Psalm 37:31

AUTHOR *Lord, why will none of his steps slide?*

FATHER As the righteous man meditates My law and My precepts they become a very part of him. Did I not say that I would cause the covenant to be written on his heart instead of upon tablets of stone?[90] When the law becomes a part of you then you do not need any man to teach you or to give you a set of rules to live by. My Spirit will teach you and He will immediately prompt you the moment you step outside My precepts. The law becomes part of you and if you will listen to the Spirit then you will know immediately if you step outside My precepts.[91] Obey the prompting of the Spirit and none of your steps will slide or waver. You have a re-programmed mind and a heart that desires to keep My word.[92] How can you go wrong if you listen to My voice within you? Indeed your ears will hear a word behind you saying, 'This is the way, walk in it', whenever you turn to the right hand or whenever you turn to the left.[93]

Psalm 37:32–33

AUTHOR *Lord, why do the wicked watch the righteous and seek to slay them?*

JESUS My people, you are on trial. The world is watching you like a hawk. You are My representatives in this earth[94] and the wicked look for any excuse not to obey Me. Therefore they look at you to see if you will keep My law and My precepts. They are ready to point the finger at any opportunity and they will delight if they see you do something which they perceive as being wrong. They will seek any and every opportunity to bring you to trial and have you put to death. But do not worry, My people, for I am with you and I will see to it that you are vindicated in the courts. Only keep close to Me and repent immediately of any mistakes that you make. Do your utmost to walk righteously with those of the world.[95] Give the enemy no opportunity and I will support you when false accusations are made against you – and they will be, for they falsely accused Me. But fear not for I will justify you in the courts of the wicked, and every tongue that rises against you in judgement I will condemn, for this is your heritage as My servants and your righteousness is of Me, says your Lord.[96]

Psalm 37:34–36

JESUS Wait on Me and keep My ways and I will exalt you, and you shall inherit the land when the wicked are cut off. You will see this. Fear not for I am coming to exalt My own. It will soon be time. Remain faithful to Me. Remain faithful to My word and do that which is right in My sight. Walk circumspectly and redeem the time[97] and I will justify you amongst the heathen. At this time it may seem that the wicked have great power. Indeed gross darkness will cover the earth[98] and the wicked will do wickedly for the night is coming. As it was in the days of Noah so it will be in these days, says the Lord. Violence and great wickedness will fill the earth and men will do just as they please.[99] But as it was in Noah's day I will say enough and I will bring judgements on this wicked generation who will not repent. Therefore hold fast and watch what I will do, for it will not be long. Indeed just as the flood came and swept them away in Noah's day[100] so will fire fall and destroy this wicked generation.[101] Hold fast, those of you who are righteous, for he who overcomes will see My glory fill the earth and the wicked shall be no more.[102]

Psalm 37:37–38

AUTHOR *Lord, what is the future of the blameless man, and who is a blameless man?*

FATHER A blameless man is the man who has given his sin to Jesus in exchange for His righteousness. When you make Jesus your Lord then He takes your sin and gives you His righteousness instead.[103] I then take your sin and remove it far from you,[104] for it is yours no longer. I cast it into the sea of forgetfulness and I remember it no more.[105] You are then blameless in My sight and your righteousness is of Me, says your Lord. The blameless man shall inherit the earth. When Jesus comes to set up His kingdom on the earth then peace shall prevail, for He is the Prince of Peace. Great will be the increase of His government and peace, and there shall be no end to it.[106] This is your future and your hope. However, he who rejects My Son shall retain his sin and he shall be wicked in My sight, and he shall be cut off from the kingdom of peace, for even his righteous deeds shall be as filthy rags in My sight.[107] You must wear a robe of righteousness to enter My kingdom,[108] and that robe is only obtainable from My Son Jesus as you come to Him in repentance and give Him your sin. If you reject Him and retain your sin then you shall be cut off from My kingdom of peace, for the wicked cannot enter it. And you are all wicked, for every one of you has sinned and fallen short of My glory.[109] There is no one who is righteous, no not one.[110] Therefore your righteousness must be of Me if you desire to inherit My kingdom and My peace.

Psalm 37:39–40

AUTHOR *Lord, what does it mean for the salvation of the righteous to be from You?*

FATHER As I said, your righteousness is from Me and not from yourselves. So also is your salvation from Me. I have given you a complete package that includes salvation from the consequences of your sin,[111] salvation from slavery to your enemy,[112] salvation from sickness,[113] salvation from disturbance of the mind,[114] salvation from poverty[115] and indeed salvation from all the works of the evil one.[116] My Son Jesus is your Salvation and He is from Me.[117] Therefore your salvation is of Me. You cannot save yourselves. If that were possible I would not have had to sacrifice My Son for you, neither would He have had to come to you. But I sent Him, and I anointed Him to preach good news to the poor, to heal the broken hearted, to preach deliverance to the captives and recovery of sight to the blind, to set at liberty those who are oppressed and to preach the year of My favour on mankind.[118] I sent Him to destroy the works of the evil one.[119] Yes your salvation is from Me for you cannot save yourselves. And My Salvation shall be your strength. He is My strong right arm and He has won for you the victory.[120] Rely on Him, put your trust in Him, and He shall deliver you from all the wiles of the enemy and from the snare of the fowler.[121] Trust in Jesus and you shall overcome, and to those who overcome I will grant the right to inherit the earth.[122]

Notes

Psalm One
(pages 11–20)

1. Phil 4:7
2. Isa 26:3
3. Prov 16:25
4. Prov 13:20
5. 1 Pet 1:15
6. Jn 6:68
7. Ps 119:105
8. Jn 16:13–14
9. Matt 16:16–18
10. Jn 7:38–39
11. Ezek 47:1, Rev 22:1
12. Ezek 47:5
13. Matt 7:24–27
14. Ezek 47:12, Rev 22:2
15. Ezek 47:9
16. Jn 5:19, 14:10
17. Eph 2:10
18. Eph 4:13–15
19. Rom 12:2
20. 2 Cor 3:6
21. Rev 5:10, Rev 20:6
22. Matt 25:14–30
23. Rev 14:4
24. 2 Cor 5:21
25. 1 Pet 1:23
26. Isa 64:6
27. Eph 2:8–9
28. Matt 22:12–13
29. Prov 3:5–6
30. Isa 55:9
31. Jer 29:11

Psalm Two
(pages 21–33)

1. Gen 6:5, Ps 14:2–3, Isa 53:6, Jer 17:9
2. Gen 3:4–6
3. Rom 6:16, 23, 2 Pet 2:19
4. Rev 12:12
5. Ps 22:30
6. Dan 11:32
7. Joel 3:10
8. Rom 8:31

9. Col 2:15
10. 2 Cor 4:4
11. 1 Tim 2:14
12. Isa 5:20, 2 Tim 3:13
13. Rev 12:9, 20:3
14. Isa 14:13, 2 Thes 2:3–4
15. Jn 1:1–3
16. Lk 10:18, Rev 12:7–11
17. Col 2:15
18. Rev 1:18
19. Matt 28:18–20, Mk 16:15–18
20. Rev 12:12
21. 1 Cor 1:20–23
22. Ps 14:1
23. Rom 1:18–21
24. Rev 19:17–21
25. 2 Pet 3:9
26. Ps 48:2
27. Jn 1:1
28. Jn 6:63
29. Heb 4:12, Ps 147:15, Ps 107:20
30. Heb 1:3
31. Lk 1:35,38
32. Jn 1:14
33. Matt 1:23
34. 2 Cor 5:21
35. Jn 17:3
36. Mat 27:46
37. Jn 3:3–16
38. Eph 1:19–20
39. Rom 8:29, Rev 1:5
40. 1 Cor 15:20
41. Rom 8:11
42. 2 Cor 5:17
43. Ps 115:16
44. 1 Tim 2:4
45. Gen 3:8–9
46. Lk 15:11–32
47. Jn 14:23
48. Jn 8:44
49. Isa 14:12–15, 2 Thes 2:3–4
50. Rev 19:17–21
51. 2 Pet 3:8–9
52. 1 Cor 15:24–25
53. Prov 1:1–7, 2 Tim 3:16–17
54. Col 1:9–12
55. Jer 31:31–34, Ezek 36:26–27
56. Phil 2:13
57. Prov 8:12–17
58. Jn 14:6
59. Act 4:12
60. Rom 10:9
61. Heb 12:2
62. Phil 2:8–11
63. Lk 12:4–5, Heb 10:30–31
64. 2 Cor 6:2
65. Deut 28:1–2
66. Isa 63:1–6, Joel 2:1, 11, 31, Zeph 1:14–18, Rev 6:15–17
67. Prov 28:20, Joel 2:12–14, Mal 3:10
68. 1 Cor 2:9, Eph 3:20
69. Rev 5:10, 20:4
70. Matt 21:42–44

71. Jn 14:6, Jn 3:14–16
72. Phil 3:8–9, Isa 64:6
73. 2 Cor 5:21
74. Ex 24:17
75. Mal 4:1
76. Eph 2:8–10
77. Eccl 9:3, Ps 14:1–3, Jer 17:9–10
78. Gen 2:17, Rom 6:23
79. 1 Tim 1:1
80. Rom 6:3–11
81. Col 3:3–4
82. Gal 2:20
83. Rom 10:13
84. Ps 49:6–8, 15
85. Matt 19:23–26
86. Matt 5:3–12
87. Jn 14:1–3
88. Lk 15:7, 10, 20–25

Psalm Three (pages 34–42)

1. Mk 13:7, 19, 23
2. Lk 21:28
3. Matt 24:8 (NIV)
4. Jn 15:20
5. Jn 16:33
6. Jn 5:24
7. Matt 5:11–12
8. Phil 4:4
9. Jer 29:11
10. Deut 31:6, 8
11. 1 Thes 5:16–17
12. Heb 12:2
13. Rev 1:8
14. Rev 2:7, 11, 17, 26, 3:5, 12, 21, 21:7
15. Ps 37:1–2
16. Isa 59:19
17. Ex 14:13–16
18. Isa 49:15
19. 2 Chr 20:15–17
20. Matt 14:29–30
21. Prov 18:10
22. Heb 13:20–21
23. Rev 21:3, 7
24. Ps 28:7
25. Ex 23:20–23
26. Ps 46:1–3
27. Rom 8:31
28. Jn 15:7
29. Matt 5:11
30. Ps 25:1–3
31. Isa 53:7
32. Eph 1:20
33. Heb 1:5
34. Phil 2:5–11
35. Prov 20:22, Rom 12:19
36. Ps 23:5, Ps 91:15, Jn 12:26
37. Lk 12:6–7
38. Deut 33:27
39. Jn 10:29, Heb 13:5
40. 2 Cor 5:7
41. Ps 19:7
42. Num 23:19
43. Ps 127:2
44. Matt 8:23–27
45. Ps 31:14–15

46. Phil 4:7
47. 1 Pet 3:15
48. 1 Jn 4:18–19
49. 1 Jn 4:4
50. Rom 8:31
51. 2 K 6:15–17
52. Ps 91:9–13
53. Isa 54:17
54. 1 Pet 5:8–9, Jam 4:7
55. Isa 59:21, Jn 12:49–50
56. Prov 18:21
57. Mk 16:17, Lk 10:17–20
58. Lk 4:1–13
59. Gal 4:7
60. Ex 14:15–16, Matt 28:18, 1 Cor 15:57
61. Eph 6:10–18
62. Isa 54:17
63. Deut 1:21
64. Josh 1:3–9

Psalm Eight (pages 43–53)

1. Phil 2:9–11
2. Jn 14:12–14
3. Heb 4:16
4. Mk 16:15–18
5. Act 4:12, Rev 12:11
6. Isa 6:1–3, Ezek 1:1–28, Rev 4:1–11
7. Ex 33:17–23
8. 1 Cor 13:12
9. Rev 21:3
10. Matt 18:1–5
11. Gen 18:14
12. Matt 21:16
13. 1 Pet 5:8
14. Gen 3:13
15. Gen 3:4–5
16. 1 Thes 5:16–17
17. Phil 4:7
18. Gen 3:1–6
19. 1 Jn 4:18
20. 2 Cor 10:4–5
21. Rom 8:31–32
22. Jn 8:44
23. Ps 19:1–3, Rom 1:18–25
24. Jn 1:12–13
25. Gen 1:26
26. Gen 3:8–9
27. 1 Jn 3:2, Rom 8:29, Col 1:15
28. Heb 1:14
29. The word translated 'angels' in verse 5 is *Elohiym* which is usually translated 'God'. The NKJ version gives this alternative in the margin.
30. Job 25:6
31. Ps 22:6
32. Eph 2:4–7
33. Rev 1:13–16
34. Rev 1:17
35. 1 Jn 3:2
36. Rom 8:18–21
37. Rom 8:29
38. Rom 8 :14–17
39. Jn 17:20–21

40. Ps 115:16
41. Eph 1:3–6
42. Gen 1:26–28
43. Isa 9:6–7
44. Matt 19:28
45. 1 Cor 15:20–26
46. Isa 65:17, Rev 21:1
47. Ps 37:11, Mat 5:5
48. Rev 21:3–4
49. Hab 2:14

Psalm Fourteen (pages 54–64)

1. Gen 6:5
2. 2 Thes 2:11–12
3. Gal 6:7–8
4. 1 Cor 1:19–21
5. Rom 1:20–25
6. Rom 2:3–10
7. Act 14:17
8. Rom 1:18–20
9. 1 Cor 15:3–8, Heb 12:1
10. Jn 5:36
11. Ex 3:13–14
12. Rev 1:8
13. Jer 23:23–24, Act 17:26–28
14. Rom 10:6–11
15. Jer 31:31–34, Ezek 36:26–27, Rom 8:16, 2 Cor 5:5, Eph 1:13–14
16. Isa 55:8–9
17. Isa 28:16–17, Amos 7:7–8
18. Gal 3:19–25
19. Matt 5:17
20. 1 Cor 1:30, Phil 3:9
21. 2 Cor 5:21
22. Jn 1:12–13
23. 2 Cor 5:17
24. Rom 8:16–17
25. Phil 3:20
26. 2 Cor 5:20
27. 1 Pet 2:9
28. Eccl 9:3, Jer 17:9
29. Num 14:18, 2 Chr 16:9
30. Ezek 18:23, 31–32, 33:11, 1 Tim 2:4
31. Jn 6:44
32. Deut 4:29, Matt 7:7
33. 2 Chr 15:2, Jam 4:8
34. Rom 10:8–10
35. Col 1:19–22
36. Rev 20:10, 15
37. Gen 22:14, Ps 34:9–10, Phil 4:19
38. Gen 1:28–29, 2:9, 15–17
39. Gen 2:19–20
40. Gen 3:1–6
41. Matt 7:11, Jam 1:17
42. Rom 1:28
43. Jer 17:7–8
44. Ps 34:8–10, Ps 36:7–8
45. Jn 10:10
46. Ps 37:3–4
47. Lk 12:13–21
48. Job 31:16–23, Prov 22:22–23
49. Matt 6:19–21
50. Deut 8:18

51. Gen 13:2
52. 1 Tim 6:9–10
53. Matt 6:24
54. Prov 19:17, 28:27, Lk 6:38, 2 Cor 9:6–11
55. Gen 12:1–3
56. Gal 3:13–14
57. 2 Cor 8:8–15
58. Jam 1:27
59. Matt 6:33
60. Prov 10:2, 11:4–6, 13:11
61. Job 27:16–17, Prov 13:22, 28:8
62. Ps 68:5, 146:9
63. Lk 2:25–32
64. Rom 11:25–26
65. Matt 23:39
66. Zech 12:10, Rev 1:7
67. Deut 30:3–5
68. Deut 7:9
69. Lev 18:26–28
70. Gen 17:8
71. Zech 9:9, Matt 21:1–11
72. Rev 19:11

Psalm Fifteen (pages 65–82)

1. Ex 29:43–46
2. Ex 34:29–35
3. Ex 33:11
4. Jer 31:31–34
5. 1 Cor 3:16–17
6. Matt 27:51
7. Heb 10:19–20
8. Jn 1:12–13
9. Rom 8:9–11
10. Jn 14:23
11. Jn 14:16–18
12. Jn 17:20–23
13. Rom 12:2
14. Ezek 36:26–27
15. 2 Cor 12:9–10
16. Isa 30:21
17. Zech 4:6
18. Ps 138:8, Jude 24
19. Jn 14:6
20. Rom 12:2
21. Matt 12:37
22. Matt 12:34–35
23. Col 3:16
24. Jn 12:50
25. Jn 5:19
26. 1 Cor 11:1
27. Jam 3:5–8
28. Mk 11:23
29. In Greek mythology, Dionysus the god of wine, offered to grant King Midas of Phrygia anything he wished. The king asked for everything he touched to be turned to gold. He soon came to regret his choice.
30. Prov 18:21
31. Jam 3:8–12
32. Gen 1:27
33. Gen 1:3
34. Jam 3:2–4

35. Ps 19:14, Eph 5:19–21
36. Matt 12:36
37. Num 13:25–33, 14:1–10, 26–38
38. Lk 10:25–37
39. Matt 22:34–40
40. 1 Jn 4:7–21
41. Lev 19:16, Prov 18:8, 20:19, 1 Tim 5:13
42. Prov 11:13, 16:27–28, 17:9
43. Jam 3:5–6
44. Prov 6:16–19
45. 1 Pet 2:9
46. 1 Jn 2:15–17
47. Rom 12:2
48. Matt 6:24
49. 1 Pet 1:13–16
50. 1 Cor 6:20
51. Rom 6:15–23
52. 2 Cor 11:2
53. Jn 8:42–44
54. 1 Tim 2:3–4
55. Matt 13:13–17, 2 Cor 4:3–4
56. 1 Cor 11:1
57. Matt 5:37
58. Num 23:19
59. Ps 89:34
60. Eph 1:4–12
61. Matt 26:39–44
62. Jam 1:17
63. Matt 10:8
64. Prov 13:22
65. Job 27:16–17, Prov 28:8, Eccl 2:26, Isa 60:5 The church has been grafted into Israel (Rom 11:17–18) and the wealth of the unbelievers (Gentiles) will also come to spiritual Zion, the church.
66. 1 Tim 5:17–18
67. Lev 25:35–38
68. 1 Tim 6:9–10
69. Matt 6:33
70. Gen 8:22
71. Gal 6:7
72. Lk 6:38
73. Jn 6:1–14
74. Deut 23:19–20
75. Matt 25:14–30
76. Deut 8:18
77. Jam 3:8–10
78. Prov 6:12–15
79. 1 Thes 5:11
80. Prov 16:27
81. Prov 18:8
82. Matt 18:15–17
83. 1 Cor 6:1–8
84. Gal 6:1, Jam 5:19–20
85. Eph 2:8–10
86. Phil 2:12–13
87. Matt 7:1–5
88. Rom 14:4, 10, Jam 4:11–12
89. Prov 11:13, 20:19
90. Job 12:13, Ps 73:22–25, Prov 8:12–14
91. 2 Tim 3:12–13

92. Isa 6:5–7
93. Jn 17:21
94. Ps 133
95. Eph 4:1–6
96. Eccl 4:9–12, Matt 12:25
97. Ps 37:23–24, Prov 24:16
98. Rom 14:4
99. 1 Cor 6:9–10, Gal 5:19–21, Rev 21:8

Psalm Nineteen (pages 83–99)

1. Rom 1:18–23, Act 14:17
2. Ps 46:10
3. Ps 139:7–12
4. Gen 1:14–18
5. Jn 8:12
6. Rev 21:23–24
7. Isa 9:2
8. Rev 1:16
9. Matt 24:29–30
10. Jn 11:25–26
11. Act 17:28, Col 1:17
12. Lk 1:76–79, Rev 22:16
13. Mal 4:2
14. Eph 6:17, Rev 19:15, 21
15. Isa 28:17, Amos 7:8
16. 1 Cor 1:30
17. Matt 24:27
18. Rev 1:7
19. Eccl 12:14, Mk 4:21–22
20. Jn 12:35–36
21. Mal 4:1
22. Eph 5:8, 1 Thes 5:5
23. Mal 3:2–3
24. Zech 13:9
25. Jn 17:17, Ps 119:160
26. Ps 12:6 (The number 7 represents completion and perfection).
27. Num 23:19
28. Ps 119:105, 130
29. Josh 1:7–8
30. Isa 55:8–9
31. 1 Pet 5:8
32. Jn 10:10
33. Act 9:5
34. Mal 3:10
35. Ps 119:165
36. Prov 3:5–6
37. Deut 4:10
38. Act 5:1–11
39. Isa 30:25–26, Hag 2:9 (Rivers and streams speak of the outpouring of the Holy Spirit, the anointing; and the light of the sun, the glory of God – Isa 60:1–3)
40. Joel 2:23
41. Rom 8:1
42. Prov 2:1–9
43. Jam 1:17, 2 Cor 8:9
44. Ps 119:93
45. 1 King 3:3–14
46. 1 King 11:1–13
47. Prov 10:22
48. 1 Pet 5:2
49. Jn 8:44

50. Gen 3:1–5, Matt 4:3
51. 2 Cor 11:14
52. Isa 30:21
53. Prov 3:1–2
54. Ps 91:3
55. Deut 28:1–14
56. Matt 7:24–27
57. Jer 17:9
58. Gen 3:4–5
59. Jn 12:40, 2 Cor 4:3–4
60. Jn 16:7–8
61. Rom 3:10
62. 1 Jn 3:8
63. Jn 3:17, 1 Tim 2:3–4
64. 1 Jn 2:2
65. Isa 53:4–6
66. 2 Cor 5:21
67. Eph 2:5–6
68. 1 Jn 1:8–2:2
69. Jn 1:12–13
70. 2 Cor 11:2
71. 1 Cor 6:11, Rev 1:5
72. 1 Jn 1:8–9
73. Heb 10:26–29
74. 1 Jn 3:9
75. Rom 2:4
76. 2 Cor 7:8–10
77. Rom 8:1
78. 2 Tim 3:16–17
79. Phil 2:5–8
80. Rom 12:2
81. 2 Cor 10:5
82. Jam 1:13–15
83. Rom 12:2
84. Matt 12:34–37
85. Mk 11:23
86. Jn 14:15–18, 26
87. Rom 14:4
88. Ps 40:2, Matt 7:24
89. Ps 138:8
90. Ps 1:1–3
91. Jude 24–25

Psalm Twenty-two (pages 100–140)

1. Lk 22:39–46
2. Jn 1:1, 14
3. Phil 2:5–8
4. Jn 16:13
5. Gen 2:17, Rom 6:23
6. Jn 3:3–8
7. Rom 8:8–11, 1 Cor 6:17
8. Jn 17:21
9. Gen 1:26, Deut 6:4, 1 Jn 5:7
10. Ex 3:14, Jn 8:58
11. Lk 22:44
12. Matt 26: 38–39
13. 2 Cor 5:21
14. Matt 27:45
15. Jn 17:3
16. Matt 27:45–46
17. Heb 2:9
18. Jn 3:18–21
19. Jn 8:12
20. Jn 14:6
21. Deut 30: 15, 19
22. Matt 4:11
23. Matt 26:53

24. Job 33:22, 28, Jonah 2:6
25. Heb 9:27
26. Matt 25:46, Rev 20:15
27. Rom 10:8–13
28. 2 Cor 6:1–2
29. Eph 1:4–5
30. Rom 6:23
31. Ps 103:12
32. 2 Cor 5:21
33. Heb 10:19–22
34. Rev 10:5–7
35. Matt 22:12–13
36. 2 Cor 4:3–4
37. Matt 13:13–15
38. Isa 6:3, Rev 4:8
39. Isa 6:1–5, Ezek 1, Rev 4
40. Eph 1:19–21, 2:1–7
41. Col 1:22
42. Act 4:12
43. Rom 11:17
44. Isa 66:1
45. Eph 2:20–22
46. Num 23:19, Josh 21:45
47. Jam 1:17
48. Lk 23:46
49. Heb 13:5
50. Ps 89:34
51. Heb 9:11–15
52. Jn 1:1–3, Col 1:16
53. Isa 14:12–15, Ezek 28:12–17
54. Rom 5:12
55. Phil 2:5–8
56. Jn 1:10–11
57. Matt 27:38–44
58. 1 Cor 2:7–8
59. Eph 2:4–6
60. Rev 5:9–14
61. Rev 1:18
62. Rev 1:1–2
63. Ps 37:1–11
64. Heb 12:2
65. Matt 5:44
66. Phil 2:5–8
67. Jn 5:19–20
68. 1 Pet 5:8–9
69. Jn 12:31
70. Lk 4:5–7
71. 2 Cor 5:21
72. Jn 1:29, Ex 12:5
73. Col 2:15
74. Rev 1:18
75. Matt 28:18
76. Rom 8:37
77. Mk 16:17–18
78. Ex 29:41
79. Lev 17:11–14
80. Phil 2:17, 2 Tim 4:6–7
81. 2 King 4:1–7
82. Jn 19:30
83. Lk 23:40, Matt 27:54
84. Matt 16:16–18
85. 1 Cor 2:7–8
86. 1 Cor 15:54–57
87. Ex 15:2
88. Ps 71:4–5
89. Ps 3:3–4
90. Ps 138:7
91. Ps 40:1–3
92. 1 Pet 2:9

93. Deut 30:19
94. Jn 14:6
95. Jn 11:24–26
96. Act 4:12
97. Jam 1:17
98. Jn 3:16
99. Jn 17:3
100. Jn 10:17–18
101. Matt 3:17
102. Jn 14:21
103. Deut 28:1–14
104. Eph 2:1–7
105. Gal 2:20
106. Col 3:3–4
107. Ps 3:3–4
108. Eph 1:19–21
109. Jn 10:29
110. Matt 15:24
111. Rom 10:21
112. Rom 11:11
113. Lk 24:44
114. Rom 11:25–26
115. Zech 12:10, Rev 1:7
116. Rev 1:5, Rom 8:29
117. Jn 16:15
118. Jn 4:21–24
119. Matt 7:21–23
120. Rom 2:26–29, 4:9–12
121. 1 Jn 4:8
122. Lk 15:20
123. 2 Chr 16:9
124. Isa 53:3–5
125. Rom 1:18–21
126. 1 Cor 1:18–25
127. Jn 14:7–11
128. Jn 12:32
129. Jn 14:6
130. 1 Pet 2:9
131. Matt 5:6
132. Isa 60:1–2
133. Mal 4:2
134. Jn 6:35
135. Jn 4:14
136. Isa 55:1–3
137. Jn 11:25
138. Matt 25:41, Rev 20:15
139. Matt 25:34, Rev 21:1–8
140. Matt 6:13
141. Matt 5:5
142. Rom 6:23
143. Gal 2:20
144. Eph 1:19–20
145. Phil 2:9–11
146. 2 Cor 4:3–4
147. 1 Tim 2:4
148. Matt 25:31–46
149. 1 Cor 15:24–26
150. Rev 21:1
151. Rev 20:1–3
152. Rev 20:15
153. Rev 20:7–10
154. Matt 5:1–10
155. 1 Cor 15:54–57
156. Rev 21:2–7

Psalm Twenty-three (pages 141–154)

1. Jn 10:1–18
2. Matt 6:25–34

3. Isa 54:17
4. Jer 29:11
5. Prov 3:5–6, Isa 30:21
6. Gen 2:2
7. Eccl 3:1
8. Josh 1:8, Ps 1:1–3
9. Jn 14:26
10. Isa 30:15
11. Ps 46:10
12. Isa 40:28–31
13. Rev 2:7
14. 2 Thes 3:13
15. Rom 12:2
16. Heb 12:2
17. Matt 7:24
18. 2 Cor 11:2
19. Jn 14:1–6
20. Rev 14:4
21. Matt 13:7, 22
22. Matt 18:10–14
23. Eph 5:25–27
24. Matt 7:13–14
25. Isa 30:21
26. Rev 20:10
27. Isa 14:12–15
28. Rev 12:7–10
29. 2 Cor 4:3–4
30. Jn 5:24
31. Heb 2:9
32. 1 Cor 15:54–57
33. Rom 8:35
34. Isa 11:1
35. Ps 18:30–33
36. Josh 1:8
37. Rom 12:2
38. Col 3:16
39. Ps 22:12–13, 16
40. Eph 6:17
41. Matt 4:3–4
42. Eph 6:12
43. Josh 1:8, Deut 28:8
44. Deut 23:5
45. Phil 4:19
46. Isa 50:7–8
47. Jn 6:31–35, 1 Pet 2:2
48. Jn 4:13–14, 7:37–39
49. Phil 4:15–19
50. 2 Cor 9:6–11
51. Act 10:38, Act 1:8
52. Rom 12:2, 1 Cor 2:16
53. Lk 24:49
54. Lk 11:9–13
55. Act 5:15
56. Isa 10:27
57. Ex 33:18–19
58. Jam 1:17
59. Rom 6:23
60. Isa 53:4–12
61. Deut 28:2
62. Rev 21:3
63. Eph 2:20–22
64. Rev 21:3
65. Isa 65:25
66. Rev 21:4

Psalm Twenty-four
(pages 155–168)

1. Ps 115:16
2. Gen 1:28

3. Gen 3:1–7 By disobeying God and obeying Satan, Adam effectively bowed the knee to him and made Satan the ruler of the earth. (Lk 4:5–7)
4. Act 20:28, 1 Cor 6:20
5. Eph 1:13–14
6. Matt 28:18–20, Mk 16:15–18
7. 1 Cor 15:24–25
8. Ezek 14:13, Hos 4:1–3
9. 2 Chr 7:14
10. Isa 53:6
11. 2 Pet 3:13, Rev 21:1
12. Ps 132:13–14
13. Ps 48:1–2
14. 1 Chr 21:18, 2 Chr 3:1
15. Gen 22:1–2
16. Gen 22:13–14
17. Ps 2:6–9
18. Matt 23:37–39
19. Zech 1:14–15
20. Zech 12:2–3, 9
21. Isa 65:25
22. Jer 23:5–6
23. Eph 2:20–22
24. 2 Cor 7:1
25. Matt 5:14–16
26. Isa 60:1–3
27. 1 Pet 2:9
28. Ex 24:17, Mal 4:1
29. Mal 3:2
30. Rom 3:23
31. 2 Cor 5:21
32. Rom 6:3–6, Gal 2:20
33. Col 3:3
34. Act 17:28
35. Jn 11:25
36. 2 Cor 6:2
37. Isa 64:6
38. Act 4:12
39. Heb 9:11–14
40. Eph 2:8–9
41. Rom 6:23
42. Rom 3:21–26
43. 1 Cor 2:9
44. Rom 8:17, Eph 1:11
45. Col 1:16
46. 1 Cor 1:30
47. 1 Pet 2:24
48. Phil 4:7
49. Jam 1:17
50. Eph 1:3
51. 3 Jn 2
52. Phil 4:19
53. Rom 11:1–2, 5, 25–26
54. Zech 12:10
55. Matt 23:37–39
56. 2 Cor 3:12–16
57. Isa 11:1, Rom 11:17–18
58. Gen 12:3
59. Matt 6:33
60. Gal 3:28
61. Deut 22:15, 25:7
62. Rev 19:11–16
63. Isa 40:1–5
64. Ps 73:24, Prov 19:20
65. Isa 55:6–9
66. Rev 3:20

67. Matt 24:30
68. Ps 1:1
69. Heb 12:2
70. Ps 2:6
71. Zech 9:9
72. Rev 19:11–16
73. Rev 19:17–21
74. Isa 61:2
75. 2 Thes 1:6–8
76. Ps 89:11–16
77. Ps 9:7–8
78. Josh 5:13–15
79. Ps 44:3, Isa 40:10
80. Heb 1:2–3
81. Jn 1:1–3, 14
82. Matt 17:5
83. Ex 6:3
84. Ex 3:14
85. Gen 2:4
86. Jn 5:23
87. 1 Jn 2:23
88. Hab 2:14
89. Isa 13:9–13
90. Isa 53:3
91. Ps 2
92. Matt 3:1–3

Psalm Thirty-three (pages 169–186)

1. Ps 40:2
2. Jn 16:23
3. 2 Cor 11:2
4. Eph 2:6
5. Eph 1:3
6. Act 2:38–39
7. 2 Cor 5:17
8. Rom 8:14–17
9. 1 Thes 5:16–17
10. Phil 4:4
11. Gen 1:27
12. Rev 5:8–9, 8:1–2
13. Ps 150
14. 1 Cor 14:15, Eph 5:19–20
15. Rev 5:9
16. Ezek 28:17
17. Ps 8:2
18. Gen 1:3
19. Heb 1:3
20. Col 1:15–17
21. Rev 5:11–12, 7:11–12
22. Ezek 28:12–19
23. Ps 98:9, Prov 1:3
24. Ps 145:17
25. Isa 28:17
26. Ps 119:142, 151
27. Ps 10:14–18, Ps 146:9
28. Ps 82:3–4, Isa 1:17
29. Jn 1:1–3
30. Heb 11:1
31. Gen 1:3
32. Isa 5:11
33. Mk 11:23–24
34. Matt 12:34–37
35. Ps 24:1
36. Heb 1:3, Col 1:17
37. Hos 4:1–3, 2 Chron 7:14
38. 2 Pet 3:13
39. Ex 3:13–14, 6:2–3
40. Isa 6:1–5, Ezek 1:28–2:1

41. Ex 20:18–21
42. Rom 8:16–17
43. Ps 37:11, Matt 5:5
44. Eph 3:21
45. Ps 2:1–3
46. Matt 5:18
47. Ex 4:21, 11:9–10
48. Act 8:3–4
49. Rom 6:16
50. Job 5:12
51. Matt 6:10
52. Deut 4:5–8
53. Deut 28:15–68, Isa 24:5–6, Ezek 14:13, Hos 4:1–3
54. Deut 28:1–14, 2 Chron 7:14
55. 1 Tim 2:1–2
56. Ps 139:13–16
57. Heb 4:12–13
58. Matt 6:4
59. Rom 6:23, Act 20:28
60. Ps 61:3
61. Ps 18:2
62. Isa 59:1
63. Jer 32:17
64. 2 Chron 16:7–9
65. Jer 50:34
66. Ps 91:3
67. Ps 46:1
68. 1 Pet 5:7
69. Lk 10:17–18
70. Rom 8:31
71. Ps 91:9–13
72. Num 14:18

Psalm Thirty-four (pages 187–203)

1. Ps 51:17
2. Jn 1:12–13, Rom 8:16
3. Dan 9:3, 23, 10:12–13
4. Matt 13:10–17, Rev 2:7
5. Deut 7:9
6. 1 Jn 4:8, 17–19
7. Num 23:19
8. Josh 21:45
9. Rom 8:31
10. 2 Tim 1:7
11. Ex 34:29–30
12. Act 6:15, 7:55–56
13. Isa 53:4–6
14. Jn 3:17–21
15. Heb 10:26–31
16. Ps 91:11
17. Ps 103:20–21, Heb 1:13–14
18. 2 King 6:14–18
19. Matt 26:53
20. Mal 3:10
21. Deut 28:1–2
22. Gen 3:17–19
23. Rom 8:18–23
24. Deut 28:3–14
25. Deut 28:15–68
26. Jn 14:26
27. Jn 16:13–15
28. Ps 91:14–16
29. Jam 3:5–6
30. Prov 18:21
31. Jam 3:2–4

32. Jam 3:8–12
33. Matt 5:37
34. Prov 15:4
35. Matt 4:5–6
36. 2 Tim 2:15
37. Rom 12:2
38. Isa 30:21
39. Rom 10:4, Gal 3:24–25
40. Rom 3:23
41. 2 Thes 2:9–12
42. Ex 4:21, 11:9–10
43. Matt 5:5
44. 1 Pet 1:13–19
45. Rom 10:13
46. 1 Tim 2:3–4
47. Isa 53
48. 2 Cor 11:22–28
49. 2 Cor 12:7
50. Jn 15:18–21
51. Isa 60:1–2
52. Ex 12:43–47, Jn 19:33
53. Gal 6:7–9
54. Rom 6:23
55. Rom 2:1–11
56. Jn 5:24
57. 2 Cor 5:21
58. Rev 20:10–15
59. Rom 3:21–26, Eph 1:7
60. 2 Cor 5:21, Eph 2:5–6

Psalm Thirty-seven (pages 204–237)

1. Ps 31:15
2. Matt 5:45
3. Gal 6:7–9
4. Matt 13:36–43
5. Matt 5:44–45
6. Eph 2:8–9
7. Heb 12:2
8. Phil 4:18–19
9. Deut 7:9
10. 2 Cor 5:18–20
11. Matt 6:8
12. Jn 14:12–14
13. 2 Thes 3:10–12
14. Jer 29:11, 1 Cor 2:9
15. Isa 64:8
16. Gen 2:7
17. Rom 9:21–23, 2 Cor 4:7
18. Jer 29:11
19. Jam 1:13–15
20. Eccl 3:1–8
21. 1 Pet 5:6–7
22. Isa 60:1–3
23. Ex 3:13–14
24. Matt 11:28–30
25. Eccl 3:1–8
26. Jn 15:7–8
27. Eccl 3:17
28. Jn 2:13–17, Mk 3:1–6
29. Eph 6:12
30. Eph 4:26–27
31. Heb 12:14–15
32. Rom 12:17–21
33. Eph 4:26
34. Eph 6:12
35. Matt 5:44
36. Matt 6:14–15
37. Rom 6:23

38. Matt 24:10 – The word translated offended is *skandalizo* which means to entrap. Satan uses the opportunity to be offended as a means of entrapping us. Matt 18:7 – the word translated offences is *skandalon* – the bait of a trap.
39. Eph 4:26
40. Rom 12:18, Matt 18:35
41. 1 Pet 5:6–7
42. Rom 12:19
43. Matt 7:1–5
44. Lk 17:1
45. Matt 5:44
46. Matt 6:14–15
47. Eccl 3:1
48. Heb 9:27
49. 2 Pet 3:9
50. Isa 66:24, Mk 9:42–44, Rev 20:11–15
51. Jn 11:21–27
52. Deut 30:19
53. Josh 24:15
54. Jer 29:11
55. Rom 10:13
56. 1 Tim 2:4
57. Heb 11:6
58. Dan 9:27
59. Rev 2:27
60. Matt 5:5
61. 2 Pet 3:10–13
62. Rev 21:1–3
63. Gen 3:13–19, Rev 22:3
64. Rev 22:16
65. Lk 1:78
66. Mal 4:2
67. Gal 6:7
68. Matt 26:52
69. Jn 3:19–21
70. Deut 8:18
71. Prov 10:22
72. Matt 25:15–21, 28–29
73. Ps 31:15
74. Col 1:22, Jude 24–25
75. Ezek 14:13, Hos 4:1–3
76. Phil 4:19
77. Jn 10:10
78. 2 Cor 5:21
79. Matt 26:27–28
80. Eph 2:4
81. Prov 11:24
82. Prov 19:17
83. 2 Cor 9:11
84. Gen 8:22
85. Gal 6:7–9
86. Isa 14:12–15, Rev 12:7–9
87. Rom 12:2
88. Josh 1:8
89. Matt 12:34–37
90. Jer 31:31–34
91. Ezek 36:26–27
92. Rom 12:2
93. Isa 30:21
94. 2 Cor 5:20
95. 1 Tim 3:7
96. Isa 54:17
97. Eph 5:15–16

98. Isa 60:2
99. Gen 6:5–7
100. Matt 24:37–39
101. Mal 4:1
102. Rev 2:26–27
103. 2 Cor 5:21
104. Ps 103:12
105. Mic 7:19, Act 3:19
106. Isa 9:6–7
107. Isa 64:6
108. Matt 22:11–13
109. Rom 3:23
110. Rom 3:10
111. Rom 6:23
112. Rom 6:17–18, Jn 8:31–36
113. Matt 8:16–17, 1 Pet 2:24
114. 2 Tim 1:7
115. 2 Cor 8:9, 2 Cor 9:8–11
116. Act 10:38
117. Matt 1:21
118. Lk 4:18–19
119. 1 Jn 3:8
120. Ps 98:1–2
121. Ps 91:1–3
122. Rev 2:25–26